Baseline: 52 Week Bible Study

Russell Walden

Copyright © 2013 Russell Walden

All rights reserved.

ISBN:1492905151
ISBN-13:9781492905158

DEDICATION

Dedicated to my wife Kitty. Without you this book would not have been published.

ACKNOWLEDGMENTS

Thanks to Sheryl Was for your tireless labor to faithfully edit this work.

Author's Preface

The Baseline was originally presented as a series of teachings in a radio broadcast in the 1990s. The material has been rewritten and refined every two years to keep it current to the times and my understanding of the prerogatives of the Kingdom in the lives of God's children.

The theme was originally "Spiritual Survival in the End Times." The premise of this book answers the question: "Leaving out all unnecessary information and doctrine, what are the essentials every believer should be familiar and conversant with in modern times?" These teachings are basic and rudimentary, but they are not simplistic or saccharine. Each subject focuses on a basic truth crafted to strengthen you inwardly and to bring outward blessing and power into your busy lives.

At the time of my original writing, the Davidian compound in Waco, Texas, was still smoldering. In matters of faith it is no longer enough to simply "be sincere." The Davidians were sincere--they were sincerely wrong.

It is no longer wise to leave the spiritual care of yourself and your loved ones solely in the hands of professional clergy. In the days we live in, God is putting His children on their own recognizance to provide the care for themselves that culturally and generationally has been the sole purview of our pastors and ecclesiastical leaders. Men and women must take responsibility for their own spiritual well-being which, unfortunately, has been abdicated to the ministry for five hundred years in the West. The result has been an anemic church with overburdened pastors, ill-equipped to sustain the religious welfare of their constituents in the pew.

As an individual, you must take responsibility for yourself. *"Examine yourself to see if you are in the faith,"* Paul wrote in 2 Corinthians 13:5. When you have ascertained your condition, do something about it. Likewise, as husbands, wives, mothers, and fathers, we have a responsibility for the spiritual care for those in our charge.

Since the Reformation all great and spiritual societies integrated a "family altar" into their homes. Even in the modern day with television, game consoles, smart phones, and the internet, this is still possible and practical. Wives and children have rejoiced and thrown their support behind the teachings presented in this volume. If you are a single parent, God will provide you the strength and grace to shepherd and nurture your children in these verities (truths) at whatever age.

You must be equipped with the basic information that provides an inventory of practical truth for yourself and your loved ones. *The Baseline* will give you that inventory. It will also provide the framework for a regular weekly time of gathering around the teaching of Scriptures. Face-to-face family time is an addicting practice. You will even find your children's friends will find excuses to sit at your feet and receive from you what they are not getting at home. We have heard it said for years that God is raising up a generation of mothers and fathers to pour love into the fatherless generations of the West. It is time for the spiritual mothers and spiritual fathers to rise up and take their rightful places--there are no shortcuts.

The Scriptures tell husbands to "wash their wives with the water of the Word" (Ephesians 5:26-27). This is not the pastor's job--this is the husband's job. Furthermore, in the day of reckoning, God is not going to ask the Sunday school superintendent why your children were not properly instructed in matters of faith. It is not the Sunday school teacher or the children's church minster who holds the first right of responsibility to instruct your children in spiritual matters--it is your job. The only positive reason God gave for choosing Abraham as His covenant partner is found in Gen. 18:19: *"For I know him, that he will command [teach] his children and his household after him, and they shall keep the way of the LORD . . ."*

One of the sweetest responses I received from this teaching was a cashier at the local grocery store. I had not met her before, but she had been receiving my weekly teachings for many months. She recognized me and paid the book a lovely compliment. "You know" she said, "I used to pray and go to church in order to be saved. Now that I've been following these studies, I do those things because I am saved!" What a blessing to see the travail of my soul in producing this work and to be satisfied by such an innocent and telling compliment. I trust that you, the reader, will likewise glean from these studies the spiritual substance to anchor and strengthen you for the rigors of the days in which we live.

Toward the end of equipping you and teaching you basic truth, I commend to you this book. With regard to respecting your time constraints and the burdens of everyday life, each teaching is brief and to the point. I trust you will find the studies helpful and empowering.

Russell E. Walden, Sr. March 2011

Chapter One: Everything Is in Jesus

Romans 8:32 *He that spared not his own Son, but delivered him up for us all, how shall he not with him also freely give us all things?*

The thought conveyed in the above Scripture represents a threshold, an entering place of Christian faith that every inquiring believer should cross. Any and every need you experience in life whether personal, emotional, or spiritual can only be fully met in Christ. Through a personal relationship with Jesus Christ, you have access to an inventory of available resources of God's glory to come down to earth and manifest in your life as answered prayer.

When we speak of a personal relationship with Jesus, we need to make certain clarifications: (1) this relationship is experiential, not doctrinal; (2) it arises from who you know, not what you know; and (3) it proceeds out of intimacy between you and God, not membership in a church or religious group. Experience with Christ is personal, or it is nothing.

The teachings of Jesus describe the induction of an individual into a relationship with the Father in an experience termed being "born again." Upon being born of God and entering into an ongoing personal relationship with the Creator, you potentially have every possible need in your life met already. The entire premise of the Scripture is that "God is" and that He cares about you in an intimate way. The Christian journey is one of exploration of His presence and exploitation at the Father's behest of all that the Cross affords.

Paul is making the observation in Romans 8:32 that if we accept that the Father gave His very Son in answer to our most dire need, it only follows He is certainly willing to address our lesser needs as well. In other words, in view of the belief God sent His Son to meet our greatest need, it follows that every lesser need will also be met. As a result, we may expect every honest, legitimate prayer already has an affirmative answer waiting to be dispensed at the occasion of our request.

We may conclude that the sacrifice of Christ is actually the measurement of God's willingness to act on our behalf. This willingness is a past decision the Father made and not an ongoing decision regarding every individual request. With each of your daily prayers, God does not decide whether or not He is going to honor the promise He has already made. The Father decided to be your benefactor and reflected that decision in the death, burial, and resurrection of Christ. Everything God can give you He has given you in His Son, Jesus Christ. If this is so, the common objection to this thinking is why are so many needs going unmet in the believer's life? These promises may indeed be contrary to your everyday experience, but it is totally in line with the Word of God. The first question to answer is not, "Am I experiencing God's promises?" but "Are these certain promises of God soundly offered in the Scriptures?" If we are not experiencing the receipt of those promises, we cannot turn around and hold the legitimacy of the promise up to the contradiction of our experience. Which is the rule of faith--the Scriptures or your experiences?

No doubt you have many contradictions to the positive promises of God in your life. Past experience does not determine the viability of the promises of God. If we ascertain a promise of God in the clear wording of Scripture, it does not matter if no one on earth has ever received that promise. The failure of experience does not negate the clarity of God's promises or provisions as delineated in His Word. Therefore, we must hold up the authority of the Scripture above the authority of experience in our thinking. We must take great care not to explain away the promises of God in an effort to reconcile our human experience to His divine promise. God sent His Son to give us the scope of His willingness to answer prayer. If He gave His only Son before we had the opportunity to pray our first prayer, how much more is He willing to meet our common everyday needs if we ask?

Experiences change daily, yet the Word of God is the same yesterday, today, and forever. You must anchor your sense of trust and hope in life to the promise of God and not to the variable, unstable ebb and flow of life's ups and downs. The Word of God will dominate your life as you give yourself over to it in the meditation of the Scriptures, in prayer, and in pursuit of the person and presence of Jesus Christ. Our verse then for this study is:

Romans 8:32 *He that spared not his own Son, but delivered him up for us all, how shall he not with him also freely give us all things?*

Consider this again. If God gave His only Son for your sake, is there any lesser gift He would withhold from you? Jesus is everything to the Father. In giving Jesus to you, the Father has proved to you His willingness to give you any other gift; this applies to gifts of spiritual strength and also to natural concerns such as health and material needs.

III John 2 *Beloved, I wish above all things that thou mayest prosper and be in health, even as thy soul prospereth.*

Doubts often arise when you are in prayer concerning God's willingness to meet a need. Commonly, the phrase *"if it be thy will"* is thrown in just in case you might ask for something God does not want you to have. But, if you are asking for something already promised, there is no need to add in the qualifier *"if it be thy will."* The Father gave His Son to you. Why would He withhold any lesser need? It is counterintuitive to think that the God who gave His Son is somehow reluctant to act in lesser ways on your behalf. Many will not even ask for things they believe are too trivial to bother the Lord. The common saying is, "God expects you to take care of the little things." Regardless, the Scriptures clearly state that the Lord's concern for you covers every area of life, even the so-called trivial things.

Psalm 84:11 *For the LORD God is a sun and shield: the LORD will give grace and glory: no good thing will he withhold from them that walk uprightly.*

He will not withhold any promise from you if you will just ask and trust for an answer. Those who successfully transact with God in prayer are those who have a personal relationship with Him based on intimate experience and ratified by the Scriptural record. You must pray to Him in the context of a relationship of fidelity with the Son. The promise in this verse is to those *"who walk uprightly."*

How do we walk uprightly before the Lord? In the Old Testament this meant someone who kept the Law of Moses. In the New Testament, however, righteousness is not based upon religious or moral performance but solely upon an active relationship to the Lord Jesus Christ. You are upright before God if you believe and commit your life to His person, His purpose, and His Word.

The following verse tells us God accepts us--not on the basis of what we have done or who we are, but on the basis of who Jesus is and what He has done for us in His death, burial, and resurrection.

1 Corinthians 1:30 *But of him are ye in [relationship to] Christ Jesus, who of God is made unto us wisdom, and righteousness, and sanctification, and redemption.*

Consider the implications of the above verse. It is stating that righteousness is not based on our actions (good or bad) but upon something God made Christ to become on our behalf. Our righteousness is a person (Jesus) and is activated in our relationship with Him. Our righteousness is not performance-based (keeping a set of rules). God made Jesus to be our righteousness, and our righteousness is a person.

You might ask, "Doesn't it matter how we live our lives?" Since Jesus is our righteousness, is it acceptable to live our lives in any way we please? This question has been asked since the early days of the church. Which comes first, obedience to God or the blessing of God in Christ? Unless you receive the righteousness of God that is in Christ, you have to realize moral and right living will elude you. But, if you truly appropriate what the cross of Christ affords us, this righteousness or the character of Christ will be produced in your life by virtue of the influence of God on your heart.

What are the ramifications of this relationship-based (rather than performance-based) righteousness? The implications are very practical and touch you every day in the context of your committed, personal relationship to Him as a believer. The work of Christ on the cross puts you in the position that God answers your prayer--not because of who you are or what you have done but because of who Jesus is and what Jesus has done. In Romans 5:19 Paul put it this way.

Romans 5:19 *" For as by one man's disobedience [failure to perform] many were made sinners, so by the obedience [performance] of one shall many be made righteous."*

The entire human race was judged because of Adam's sin. We were not born yet, so we did not do anything to deserve the curse of sin and death. You were doomed by Adam before you were born; however, your deliverance was also provided by Jesus before you were born.

When did Jesus' obedience justify you? Your justification was secured when He obeyed His Father and agreed to give Himself on your behalf before coming to earth. God made provision for your acceptance into the privileges of the Kingdom before you were born. You appropriate that provision when you believe the Gospel and accept Jesus as your personal Savior. Your right standing or your right to bring prayer before the Father in expectation of an answer was arranged and secured for you by Jesus on the cross; therefore, you can do business with the Father now in the midst of your circumstance because Jesus did business with the Father 2000 years ago.

Because of Jesus' obedience to God, your blessing and deliverance (laid in store since the cross) are provided and available today. Receiving answers to prayer from God has nothing to do with religious striving but in patient believing and resting in what Jesus has already accomplished on your behalf. As His heir, you are spending the rewards of Jesus' faithful service to His Father during His earth walk.

2 Peter 1:3 *According as his divine power hath given unto us all things that pertain unto life and godliness, through the knowledge of him that hath called us to glory and virtue.*

There are two provisions mentioned in this verse: One is God's provision for your godliness (i.e., *". . . all things pertaining to godliness . . .")* and the other is His arrangement for your everyday life (i.e., *". . . all that that pertain to life . . .").* Some suggest that God's interest is only in your spiritual life. They insist you should not bother Him with life's everyday troubles. But the promise of the Scriptures is that He is as committed to your natural affairs, your finances, your health, your family affairs, and employment as He is with your spiritual condition. God wants you to know He loves you so much that He wants to be involved in meeting your every need. He wants you to know your prayers are answered even before you ask.

Matthew 6:8b *Your Father knoweth what things ye have need of, before ye ask him.*

The Father knows what you need, however, it requires your faith and prayer to effect the manifestation of the answer. Not only does the Father know your needs, but from His perspective every prayer you have ever prayed has already been answered when He sent Jesus to die on the cross for you and to be raised the third day. If you believe this, you may partake of it; if you do not believe, you may suffer as though this was not even so.

Romans 8:32 *He that spared not his own Son, but delivered him up for us all, how shall he not with him also freely give us all things?*

Notice that the above verse determines when your prayers were answered. Notice the wording is *"with Him"*; that is to say, when Jesus was given by God on the cross, any other thing you might need in addition to Christ was made provision for at that time (2000 years ago). We are believing in and drawing upon a past provision. In the mind of God and as far as He is concerned, He answered every need you will ever have the day Jesus went to the cross.

Note the wording, "*. . . how shall he not with him freely give us all things?"* This is why you pray *"in Jesus name"* or *"for Jesus sake."* You are saying to God, "Father, I know that if you would give me your only Son to save my soul, I also know that you are willing to meet this lesser need." Thank the Lord that the need is already met, and He is willing to get involved in your problem.

God set the limits on what He is willing to do for you by sending Jesus. If He would give you Jesus, He will certainly give you any lesser gift. Accept Jesus, and know you are accepting everything the Father is capable of giving and doing on your behalf. His willingness is already established in His gift of Christ. Through your personal one-on-one relationship with Jesus, He will become the answers to every need in your life--you need only to ask.

Chapter Two: The Acceptance and Approval of the Father

There is a difference between God's acceptance and God's approval. Religious legalism confuses these very different aspects of your relationship with God. God's love for you is not expressed as a matter of approval. He may not approve of some aspect of your lifestyle; nonetheless, He accepts you and loves you as His child. Paul addresses this in the following verse.

Ephesians 1:3-4 *Blessed be the God and Father of our Lord Jesus Christ, who hath blessed us with all spiritual blessings in heavenly places in Christ. (v. 4) According as he hath chosen us in him before the foundation of the world, that we should be holy and without blame before him in love.*

God sovereignly chose you and regarded you as being blameless before the world was created. Before you had a chance to sin, God looked upon you as His child. He decided you would be holy and blameless even before you heard the Gospel or thought about becoming a Christian. He extended His acceptance to you before time began in order that you might have the opportunity to earn His approval. This is the understanding that bridges the gap between grace and the law. What this tells you is that your standing and relationship to the Father is something God committed Himself to before the world was made and before you ever had an opportunity to know Him.

God first sees your life and godly character as His responsibility to provide and then your opportunity to respond. He holds Himself responsible to see that you are provided (through Christ) the resources to fulfill all His expectations. Living for God is not a matter of brute force or will power but God's sovereign provision. Your part is to give your life to Him and cooperate with the purpose He seeks to unfold in your life.

Ephesians 1:5 *Having predestinated us unto the adoption of children by Jesus Christ to himself, according to the good pleasure of his will.*

The word "adoption" in the above verse does not mean Biblically what it commonly means to us today. You were not adopted as an orphan into God's family--you were born into it. You have a native-born entitlement to the privileges of the kingdom of God if you have received the new-birth experience. The term "adoption" in Eph. 1:5 is referring to an ancient family rite in New Testament times when a father would authorize his son to do business in his family's name. The adoption Paul is speaking of is the bestowal of kingdom privilege and responsibility preplanned by God for you before the world was created. God knew you and preplanned for you to be born into the family of God and, ultimately, be authorized to do business in His name just as Jesus did the Father's business while on earth.

One definition of righteousness is, "Everything you say and do being as effective as if the Father said it or did it." Your place in the Father's family is not an earned privilege;. You are born to Kingdom privileges when you accept Jesus Christ as your Savior.

Ephesians 1:6-7 *To the praise of the glory of his grace, wherein he hath made us accepted in the beloved. (v. 7) In whom we have redemption through his blood, the forgiveness of sins, according to the riches of his grace.*

You are accepted as a child of God as a result of something the Father did for you--He made you accepted. You cannot do anything to be accepted by God other than to act in confidence that this is so. You are loved of God. You are redeemed by the blood Jesus spilled on the cross. You are accepted, loved, and redeemed by what Jesus did for you, not what you have done for him, for others, etc. You do not earn the love of God. All prayer is answered through the love of God. Grand promises and resolutions to do better do not sway the Father's favor toward your needs. His willingness to answer prayer is not because you are holy but because Jesus is holy. God blesses you, loves you, and moves in your life (not based on who you are or what you have done) based on who Jesus is and what He has done and your committed relationship to His Lordship. You cannot earn or deserve the blessing of

God. When He answers your prayer, He is giving you what Jesus earned for you on the cross. You are not getting what you deserve; you get what Jesus deserves.

Christian tradition generally teaches that a believer may only access Heaven's resources in the context of good works measured according to church standards. This is the Gospel, however, it is not church tradition. God does have a standard, but it is one that is met by those believers who are secure in their walk with God and motivated by love (not fear).

Romans 5:19 *For as by one man's disobedience many were made sinners, so by the obedience of one shall many be made righteous.*

Adam's sin caused all of man to suffer. You were not in the Garden of Eden and you never had a choice in the matter of the fall. Adam's choice brought us all under the curse of sin. Likewise, you were not on the cross with Jesus. But His obedience and His choice have made it possible for you to reap the benefits Jesus secured for you at Golgotha. God blesses you as a result of the sacrifice Jesus made and not the sacrifice Christianity or your religious thinking requires. All prayer is answered on the basis of who Jesus is and what He has done; it is your committed relationship to Him and not solely on who you are or what you have (or have not) done.

Hebrews 10:19 *Having therefore, brethren, boldness to enter into the holiest by the blood of Jesus.*

You come to the Father by the Blood and not by religious works. The blood of Christ is your claim to every promise of God. Your failures, sins, and mistakes have no bearing on your standing with God. You come to Him pleading access by the Blood rather than your virtues. You can run to His presence in full assurance that His arms are wide open to receive you on the basis of His shed blood.

Jesus paid your admission into the theater of God's grace. As a child of God, you have authority over the works of the devil, victory over sin, and a vast storehouse of blessing and promise available to you by the prayer of faith. All this comes out of God's acceptance of you and is based on who Jesus is and not who you are. You need never try to earn His acceptance; it has been blood-bought by Jesus on the cross for your benefit. However, this does not mean you can live any way you wish and expect to access Kingdom benefits. What of God's approval? It is an issue that becomes increasingly important as you grow spiritually. The Father's approval or disapproval are determining factors as to whether you will fulfill His destined purpose for you on the earth. His approval or disapproval determines whether you will experience the benefits of His perfect will or simply His permissive will.

The Father's acceptance has nothing to do with what you have or have not done. His approval, however, has everything to do with your actions, motives, and conduct in life. Even though He thoroughly disapproves of your actions, He still accepts you as His child and will deal with you as a loving Father.

Chapter Three: What It Is to Be a Child of God

All Christian religions have a base-line requirement men must fulfill in order to be blessed of God and accepted by Him. This is their creed, their "truth." Many teach that God requires great personal sacrifice as the means of securing eternal bliss. Others propose that all men are God's children and all you must give is a general assent to the "golden rule" to satisfy the divine requirement. Still others place importance on doctrinal nuances (or outward conformity) to a certain religious standard.

What is the truth? Does it matter how we live or what we believe? Is God only looking for sincerity of intent? By its very nature, truth is mutually exclusive--there can be only one truth. Yet, as we shall see in this chapter, truth is not a set of doctrines or teachable principles--truth is much, much more.

Relativism or the belief that what is true for you is not necessarily true for another is one of the greatest lies Satan has perpetuated in modern society. It is often said, "It doesn't matter what you believe, just so you are sincere. " There can only be one truth, one creator, one dogma that all men are called everywhere to embrace. The myriads of religions (even the hundreds of Christian religions) are not a tribute to God's diversity but a manifestation of man's spiritual myopia or inability to see, except, or embrace the broad perspective of the kingdom of God and the one great truth that is the underpinning of all Christian faith.

In order to sort through the varied opinions to get at the truth, you must first accept Scriptures as authoritative on all matters pertaining to the Christian walk. The word of God must be accepted as a book that always points us to Christ and contains objective truth, or the Bible becomes merely the articulation of religious principles that are merely convenient for the moment. It must be accepted that the Bible is an infallible expression of truth.

2 Peter 1:19-21 *We have also a more sure word of prophecy; whereunto ye do well that ye take heed, as unto a light that shineth in a dark place, until the day dawn, and the day star arise in your hearts: (v. 20) Knowing this first, that no prophecy of the scripture is of any private interpretation. (v. 21) For the prophecy came not in old time by the will of man: but holy men of God spake as they were moved by the Holy Ghost.*

While the Bible expresses truth, there must also be an understanding that Jesus, himself, personifies truth. The way of life Jesus came to establish in the first century was not centered on the Bible but on Himself. The Word of God expressed in the Bible is the clothing of the word of God personified in Jesus. Jesus did not die to give us a book called the Bible. He died to give us Himself and to bring us into a personal relationship with Him. Therefore, true Christianity is more a relationship than a philosophy, lifestyle, or teachable religion. You can live a Christian lifestyle, hold to its philosophy, practice Christian religion, and still not be a child of God. A personal relationship with Jesus validates you as a child of God regardless of correctness of philosophy, lifestyle, or religion. Consequently, you may conclude that a personal relationship with Jesus Christ is the minimal requirement of true Christianity. You should not stop there; it is to be accepted as fact and seen as important above all else. To have all other aspects of Christianity in full bloom in your life means nothing in the eyes of God if you are lacking in this one area. But, if you have a true relationship with Jesus, it will be impossible for you not to develop a philosophy of life, lifestyle, and religious sense pleasing to God.

If you have children, consider the basis on which you accept them--you feed, clothe, and house them because you accept them. However, you may not always approve of them. You love them and are there for them, but sometimes you need to deal with them from a position of disapproval even though you continue to accept them as your children. When your children act in disapproval, there are privileges you will withhold for the purpose of teaching discipline and setting standards for them. In fact, there are times you totally disapprove of your children's actions while in the same breath you never stop feeding, housing, or clothing them. Why? You accept responsibility for them because they are your children and you accept them as such.

Matthew 7:11 *If ye then, being evil, know how to give good gifts unto your children, how much more shall your Father which is in heaven give good things to them that ask him?*

The Father of your soul deals with you in the same way you deal with your own children. You can be totally accepted of God as His child even though He may disapprove of your lifestyle at any given point. Even though you are being disciplined, the Father still cares for you. There are basic promises and blessings that are yours simply because you are a child of God.

Matthew 6:27-29 *Which of you by taking thought can add one cubit unto his stature? (v. 28) And why take ye thought for raiment? Consider the lilies of the field, how they grow; they toil not, neither do they spin: (v. 29) And yet I say unto you, That even Solomon in all his glory was not arrayed like one of these.*

Like some parents the Father never says, “That's not my little boy; my little boy would not do thus and such.” What He says is, “You are my child, I love you, but I will not allow you to walk in my full blessing until this changes in your life.”

Hebrews 12:9-10 *Furthermore we have had fathers of our flesh which corrected us, and we gave them reverence: shall we not much rather be in subjection unto the Father of spirits, and live?(v. 10) For they verily for a few days chastened us after their own pleasure; but he for our profit, that we might be partakers of his holiness.*

The Father deals with you on two very different levels. He deals with you mutually in terms of acceptance and also approval. There are base-line benefits that accrue to you simply because you are His child

(He accepts you). Real growth and fulfillment, however, only comes as you go beyond spiritual infancy and seek His approval in your life. Your acceptance before God is secured by your new birth. The approval of the Father, therefore, is based upon obedience and ongoing submission. What then is the basis of the Father's acceptance?

1 Peter 2:5 *Ye also, as lively stones, are built up a spiritual house, an holy priesthood, to offer up spiritual sacrifices, acceptable to God by Jesus Christ.*

Your acceptability to God is secured through the person of Christ. Because of what Christ has done on the cross and who He is, you are accepted in the Father's family. You cannot diminish or augment your standing in the family of God by who you are, what you have done, or what you have not done in life. You are acceptable to God through Christ, and you are approved of God through your actions. This is the difference between the Father's acceptance and His approval.

Hebrews 11:6 *But without faith it is impossible to please him: for he that cometh to God must believe that he is, and that he is a rewarder of them that diligently seek him.*

The word for faith is "confidence." If your children did not trust you, you would be displeased. You would not disown them, but you would disapprove of that unfounded distrust. As a parent, after all your labor and work to provide a home and supply their needs, you would expect your children to have a level of trust in you. Likewise, you must understand that you meet the Father's approval through your trust in His nature and faithfulness.

There are rewards from God's hand that will be withheld from you until you begin to seek His approval in your life through developing trust in Him. At the same time, however, you are still accepted as His child, and He is providing for you on that basis. Securing God's approval involves soliciting and securing His will and direction in every area of your life. Serving the Father's purpose in your life will place you at His disposal to serve His highest purpose even if that purpose is fulfilled at your own personal expense.

Romans 10:9 *That if thou shalt confess with thy mouth the Lord Jesus, and shalt believe in thine heart that God hath raised him from the dead, thou shalt be saved.*

The sinner's prayer is based on the above Scripture. When someone becomes a Christian, this verse is the invitation he should be cited. He then makes a declaration that his life is now committed to the lordship of Jesus Christ. As a sinner, he now commits the whole of his life over to God's loving care and believes God raised Jesus from the dead (an expression of love for man).

If that prayer is prayed in utter sincerity and from the heart, there is a miracle of creation that takes place. The individual becomes "born again." From the dry husk of his dead human spirit, a new human spirit emerges, indwelling itself by the Spirit of God. The Holy Spirit within that human spirit will then go about securing the borders of that man or woman's life as the personal domain and property of the kingdom of God.

Chapter Four: Understanding Water Baptism

In the genesis of the early church, Peter stood up and articulated to the city of Jerusalem the means of extradition from the domain of darkness to the kingdom of light. One element of that passage involves the rite of water baptism. For two thousand years baptism has remained a subject of controversy. In modern times it has lost much of its significance as has the ordinance of communion. Nevertheless, water baptism remains a crucial aspect of becoming a Christian and is not wisely ignored or deemed insignificant.

Acts 2:38 *Then Peter said unto them, Repent, and be baptized every one of you in the name of Jesus Christ for the remission of sins, and ye shall receive the gift of the Holy Ghost.*

Water baptism is unique to the Christian faith. It is to Christianity what circumcision was to the ancient Jewish culture of Jesus' day. It represents a line of demarcation between the old life of sin and a new life in Christ. It is so important that Jesus (having no real need to be baptized in water) required John to baptize Him in order to "fulfill all righteousness." To properly understand baptism we must tie it in with its Old Testament counterpart--circumcision.

Genesis 17:9-11 *And God said unto Abraham, Thou shalt keep my covenant therefore, thou, and thy seed after thee in their generations. (v. 10) This is my covenant, which ye shall keep, between me and you and thy seed after thee; Every man child among you shall be circumcised. (v. 11) And ye shall circumcise the flesh of your foreskin; and it shall be a token of the covenant betwixt me and you.*

Circumcision was the outward sign of God's covenant with Abraham and the nation of Israel after Him. This outward sign of a covenant was a common cultural component in the ancient Bible lands among those who practiced the rite of the covenantal agreement. When two men would go into business together, they would customarily cut a blood covenant. The incision would be in a conspicuous place as a reminder to each party and to all concerned that these men were joined in a mutual agreement. A blood covenant in those days was more binding than marriage. You could divorce your spouse, but if you broke a blood covenant, it was an automatic death sentence.

In blood covenant the two parties allowed the blood from their cuts to flow together, thus saying that their lives were one and that all resources pertaining to each other were now joined for mutual benefit. This covenant was seen as a symbolic death of the participants' separate lives and their joining together in new lives with new families. Now, let us consider the relationship between the idea of blood covenant and water baptism.

Romans 6:3-4 *Know ye not, that so many of us as were baptized into Jesus Christ were baptized into his death? (v. 4) Therefore we are buried with him by baptism into death: that like as Christ was raised up from the dead by the glory of the Father, even so we also should walk in newness of life.*

Baptism is the act of a new Christian identifying personally with the death, burial, and resurrection of Christ. He is saying in public, "I accept the death of Christ as my death, and the resurrection of Christ as my resurrection." The death of Christ was a blood covenant death. If being baptized is identifying with the death, burial, and resurrection of Christ, then it follows that baptism is a recognition and acceptance of the covenantal aspects of those events.

The term "testament" means covenant or literally cutting. The old covenant was based on God requiring man's blood in circumcision and animal blood in sacrifice. The new covenant only requires the blood of Christ and your acceptance of that blood as a substitute for your own blood. Jesus cut both sides of the new covenant on the cross. He could accomplish this because He was both man and God.

1 Timothy 2:5 *For there is one God, and one mediator between God and* *men, the man Christ Jesus.*

Every covenant had what was known as a mediator. The mediator would appoint the time two parties would meet together to cut a covenant. Jesus was God, man, and mediator. He chose the time of His death saying, *"No man takes my life from me, I lay it down of my own accord . . ."* The mediator would officiate with the knife and the intermingling of the spilled bloods. Jesus' natural blood supply was a physical mingling of the divine life of God and the life's blood of His humanity. In the covenant of circumcision, a Levitical priest was the mediator. The Levite also mediated the spilling of animal blood in sacrifice to God (a remembrance of the covenant of circumcision).

On the cross Jesus was the mediator--He was the High Priest, He was man, and He was God. When He died, Jesus spilled the blood of both God and man in a binding contractual agreement for all eternity. The Father in heaven is bound to honor that covenant, and when individual men acknowledge that covenant, they subsequently experience the new birth and are brought into an irrevocable, eternal contract with God Himself. The terms of the contract are simple. For your part you are saying you and all that you possess are at the Father's disposal. Anything He has need of you will provide with no questions asked. Likewise, all that the Father represents in terms of resources are at your disposal (no questions asked) on the basis of the covenant.

Genesis 22:2-3 *And he said, Take now thy son, thine only son Isaac, whom thou lovest, and get thee into the land of Moriah; and offer him there for a burnt offering upon one of the mountains which I will tell thee of. (v. 3) And Abraham rose up early in the morning, and saddled his ass, and took two of his young men with him, and Isaac his son, and clave the wood for the burnt offering, and rose up, and went unto the place of which God had told him.*

Abraham did not object or utter one word here. Jehovah, his blood covenant partner, had need of his only son. He would offer him without question. God was showing us through Abraham's example the cost of the covenant with Him--absolute and total obedience. All giving to God to the church is recognizing that all we have is God's, and if we give in faith as Abraham did, we will receive back what we give even as Abraham received his son back by faith.

Acts 2:41 *Then they that gladly received his word were baptized: and the same day there were added unto them about three thousand souls.*

Being baptized is the proper response of a whole-hearted acceptance of the Gospel. Baptism is the follow-through action of someone who has already accepted Jesus as his or her Savior.

Acts 10:48 *And he commanded them to be baptized in the name of the Lord. Then prayed they him to tarry certain days.*

Baptism is performed in the name of the Lord because it is identification with what He did on the cross. It is not the act of church membership or association with a certain creed. Early church believers were joined to the church by laying on of hands as "confirmation."

Romans 6:3 *Know ye not, that so many of us as were baptized into Jesus Christ were baptized into his death?*

Being baptized is the outward act of saying, "I acknowledge that the penalty for my sins is death and, furthermore, that Jesus died a death for this reason and that His death is accepted by the Father as payment for my sins."

Romans 6:4 *Therefore we are buried with him by baptism into death: that like as Christ was raised up from the dead by the glory of the Father, even so we also should walk in newness of life.*

The acceptance of the death of Christ will bring a release of the life of God into a new Christian's experience that is described as being "born again." With this experience is a promise of great personal peace and blessing. The old human life with its vulnerabilities and limitations is washed away to a watery grave; a clean slate is given as well as a new, more than human nature. The believer becomes essentially a being along the same order as Jesus Christ when He walked the earth. He becomes a God man. He is human, indwelled, and possessed of the life and nature of God Himself.

1 Peter 3:21 *The like figure whereunto even baptism doth also now save us (not the putting away of the filth of the flesh, but the answer of a good conscience toward God,) by the resurrection of Jesus Christ.*

Finally, baptism is meant to give us a weapon against the devil when he tries to condemn us for our past. You say in effect: "The old man is dead and buried, his sins were paid for on the cross, and I refuse to be in heaviness or anxiousness over that which the death of Christ delivered me." If you have not been baptized, you must do so. Your walk with God will be deficient until there is a clear public profession of separation from the old human life and open embrace of the life and family of God.

Chapter Five: The Doctrine of Christ

2 John 9 *Whosoever transgresseth, and abideth not in the doctrine of Christ, hath not God. He that abideth in the doctrine of Christ, he hath both the Father and the Son.*

The central truth in the Bible is called the "doctrine of Christ." In all the different Christian groups, there are many teachings, practices, and philosophies. This one doctrine draws the line between what makes up a reliable body of doctrine and a teaching that is cultic. It is imperative to understand this teaching and be able to apply it to the beliefs of different faiths to which we are exposed.

Some years ago I had an experience that drove home the importance of this doctrine. A pair of clean-cut young men showed up in my front yard, parked their bicycles, and knocked on my door. I knew by their appearance they were members of a religious proselytizing group. Since these groups usually paired a new convert with a seasoned veteran, I hoped that by conversing with these men I could touch the life of the less-indoctrinated young man for Jesus. Several visits later I allowed them to leave literature. I quickly came to realize this group did not believe in Jesus as the only, unique Son of God, and during this time I developed a severe flu and could not shake it. I would feel better and leave the house, only to return home violently ill. I went to a pastor's meeting and shared my problem with a fellow minister. He showed me the following scripture:

2 John 10-11 *If there come any unto you, and bring not this doctrine, receive him not into your house, neither bid him God speed: (v. 11) For he that biddeth him God speed is partaker of his evil deeds.*

When I returned home, I took all the literature I had accepted and burned it in my fireplace. On my knees I asked the Lord to forgive me for inadvertently allowing these men into my home contrary to His Word. I was quickly healed of the sickness, and I was immediately uplifted and felt as though I had never been sick. The next day the young men returned, and as patiently as I could, I explained to them the verse about the doctrine of Christ. I told them I would pray their work would fail in my city. A short time later I heard they had moved to another area.

When people first come to the Lord, there will invariably be contact with religious proselytizing groups. This is a strategy of Satan to undermine new-found faith in Christ. The example I shared from my own life is a good example of how to deal with these persons. They should not be meddled with because they do not hold the doctrine of Christ. Below is a warning from Paul.

2 Timothy 3:14-15 *But continue thou in the things which thou hast learned and hast been assured of, knowing of whom thou hast learned them; (v. 15) And that from a child thou hast known the holy scriptures, which are able to make thee wise unto salvation through faith which is in Christ Jesus.*

Remember this: The truth heard the first time will almost always produce a negative reaction. We cannot always rely on what sounds right to judge truth or error. False teachers will always begin by telling you things that are pleasant and agreeable. John had this to say in his first letter.

1 John 4:5-6 *They are of the world: therefore speak they of the world, and the world heareth them. (v. 6) We are of God: he that knoweth God heareth us; he that is not of God heareth not us. Hereby know we the spirit of truth, and the spirit of error.*

In judging a teaching you have heard, always ask yourself: "Does this teaching honor Jesus or take honor from Him? Does it make me more dependent upon Jesus, or does it cause me to feel self-reliant or dependent on a teaching or organization? Is it 'Christo-centric' or 'Christ-centered?'" It is never comfortable to separate yourself from people or to be confrontational, but there comes a time for your own safety to draw the line. Having a firm understanding of the doctrine of

Christ is important for knowing just where to draw that line. In the next few chapters, we will explore the full dimension of the doctrine of Christ.

Chapter Six: The Doctrine of Christ: One God

2 John 9 *Whosoever transgresseth, and abideth not in the doctrine of Christ, hath not God. He that abideth in the doctrine of Christ, he hath both the Father and the Son.*

The Amplified version of the Bible will shed light on what is meant by the doctrine of Christ. *"Anyone who runs ahead of God and does not abide in the doctrine of Christ (who is not content with what He taught) does not have God. But he who continues to live in the doctrine (teaching) of Christ does have God; he has both the Father and the Son."*

The doctrine of Christ is expressed two ways. First, it is the combined truth of what Jesus taught while here on the earth. Secondly, it is the teaching concerning His person--or who is Jesus. The latter teaching is what is covered here. To comprehend who Jesus is will revolutionize your life. Peter was the first to discover the doctrine of Christ, and his confession of the person of Christ released great blessing and promise into his life.

Matthew 16:13 *When Jesus came into the coasts of Caesarea Philippi, he asked his disciples, saying, Whom do men say that I the Son of man am?*

Who is Jesus to you? Do you only see a suffering Savior? Do you see Him as the ruling Lord of the earth and, in fact, your own life? Is He merely a distant historical figure? Perhaps He is only the focus of a religious lifestyle or church affiliation. To many He is only one of several plastic icons fixed to the dashboard of their car or in a corner of their bedroom or living room. Who do you say that Jesus is to you?

Matthew 16:14 *And they said, Some say that thou art John the Baptist; some, Elias; and others, Jeremias, or one of the prophets.*

Was Jesus only a man, a contemporary with Mohammed, Confucius, or Buddha?

Matthew 16:15 *He saith unto them, But whom say ye that I am?*

Confronting his followers after all the comparisons, Jesus is still looking for the right answer. Who is Jesus? The doctrine of Christ holds that He is the unique Son of God and is unparalleled by any other religious figure in Judaism, Islam, or even Christianity itself.

Matthew 16:16-17 *And Simon Peter answered and said, Thou art the Christ, the Son of the living God. (v. 17) And Jesus answered and said unto him, Blessed art thou, Simon Barjona: for flesh and blood hath not revealed it unto thee, but my Father which is in heaven.*

"Blessed are you . . ." was Jesus instant response to Peter when Peter declared the only appropriate answer. The word *blessed* here means "happy" or "happier." To paraphrase, Jesus is saying, "Pete, you've got something to be happy about! You know who I am! And you could only have learned this from My Father in Heaven." So, the revelation of Jesus as the unique Son of God is evidence that you have been in communication with God the Father!

Matthew 16:18 *And I say also unto thee, That thou art Peter, and upon this rock I will build my church; and the gates of hell shall not prevail against it.*

Though Peter was changed as a result of this revelation, he still had much to learn, and many mistakes were ahead of him. He would become, however, just what Jesus declares of him here--a rock that the church could be grounded upon. A man who knows his Savior becomes a pillar of strength that will cause others to stand firm through the storms of life.

Matthew 16:19 *And I will give unto thee the keys of the kingdom of heaven: and whatsoever thou shalt bind on earth shall be bound in heaven: and whatsoever thou shalt loose on earth shall be loosed in heaven.*

This revelation of Jesus brings a promise of great authority.

Peter, having known now who Jesus is, will never rely on religion or on himself to produce the life and blessing of God. Once when Peter worked a miracle, he indicated his perception of where the grace of God's power proceeded from in Acts 3:12.

Acts 3:12 *And when Peter saw it, he answered unto the people, Ye men of Israel, why marvel ye at this or why look ye so earnestly on us, as though by our own power or holiness we had made this man to walk?*

It was Jesus, the Son of the Living God, who worked the healing for the lame man. It was not anything Peter had done other than believe upon Jesus and trust the Spirit of Christ to produce the answered prayer.

Acts 5:15 *Insomuch that they brought forth the sick into the streets, and laid them on beds and couches, that at the least the shadow of Peter passing by might overshadow some of them.*

Because the doctrine of Christ was written on Peter's heart, he once again went forward to give marvelous testimonies of the greatness of God.

Acts 10:34 *Then Peter opened his mouth, and said, Of a truth I perceive that God is no respecter of persons.*

There was nothing special about Peter, and he knew it. When believers come to God in humility and expectation that He will be the "Son of the Living God" in their lives, Peter loudly proclaims that what God does for one He will do for anyone.

1 Timothy 2:5 *For there is one God, and one mediator between God and men, the man Christ Jesus;*

This verse of Scripture is one the simplest expressions of the doctrine of Christ in the fewest words. There are three parts to the doctrine of Christ:

1. There is *one* God;

2. There is *one* Mediator; and

3. The *man* Christ Jesus.

We do not have three gods--we have one God. This is a great mystery in the Bible.

1 Corinthians 8:6 *There is but one God, the Father and one Lord Jesus Christ.*

This being so, then how do the Father and Son relate to one another?

John 10:30 *I and my Father are one.*

There is the Father, the Son, and the Spirit, but they are one. Nowhere in the Bible is this explained fully. We must take this truth on faith and not analysis it to be true. How is it that God can be three and yet one? Perhaps it can be expressed in this way: "I am a father to my children, a husband to my wife, and a pastor to my flock. I am one person, but I have multiple roles I fulfill." The book of Genesis tells us that man is made in the image of God.

Genesis 1:26 *And God said, Let us make man in our image, after our likeness: and let them have dominion over the fish of the sea, and over the fowl of the air, and over the cattle, and over all the earth, and over every creeping thing that creepeth upon the earth.*

Genesis 9:6 *Whoso sheddeth man's blood, by man shall his blood be shed: for in the image of God made he man.*

If you want to understand God's nature, look at His image. Man has a spirit, a soul, and a body. These three elements are different and distinct, however, they make up one man when combined together. Man is three, yet he is one. If you remove one part, he is not man but animal. God is Father, Son, and Spirit. If you remove one part, He is not God. He is three, yet He is one--the Father is God, the Son is God, and the Holy Spirit is God.

1 Timothy 3:16 *And without controversy great is the mystery of godliness: God was manifest in the flesh, justified in the Spirit, seen of angels, preached unto the Gentiles, believed on in the world, received up into glory.*

This study does not seek to explain God but to encourage you to accept Him on His own terms in the manner in which He has chosen to reveal Himself to us. There is *one* God, there is *one* Mediator, the *man* Christ Jesus.

Chapter Seven: One Mediator

***We have covered the importance of the doctrine of Christ and shown it has three elements seen in this Scripture:

1 Timothy 2:5 *For [there is] one God, and one mediator between God and men, the man Christ Jesus.*

The doctrine of Christ is:

There is one God

There is one Mediator

The man Christ Jesus

The Greek word for "mediator" is used five more times in the New Testament. Letting Scripture interpret Scripture, we can learn what a mediator is and how Jesus is our mediator. Here is the definition of the Greek word "mediator": *One who intervenes between two, either in order to make or restore peace and friendship, or form a compact, or for ratifying a covenant; a medium of communication, arbitrator.* If Jesus is your mediator, then He has intervened between you and God. Why was this necessary?

Ephesians 2:12 *. . . ye were without Christ, being aliens . . . having no hope, and [being] without God in the world.*

We are all born separated from God by sin. Sin's effect in our lives causes us to suffer as though there were no God on the earth.

Colossians 1:21 *And you, that were sometime alienated and enemies in [your] mind by wicked works, yet now hath he[Jesus] reconciled.*

Jesus intervened between God and man; between the two, peace and friendship were restored. The work of Jesus on the cross is the basis of your approach to God. Jesus was the go-between. On the cross He did away with any hindrance restraining man from being in perfect fellowship with the Father in heaven. Apart from Christ, our good works could never close the gap between God and ourselves. Jesus became a bridge of faith for us. All who accept Him as Lord and Savior may cross over and come into the "kingdom of love and light."

Colossians 1:13 *Who hath delivered us from the power of darkness, and hath translated [us] into the kingdom of his dear Son.*

Through the work of Jesus on the cross, it has become possible for you to be "translated" (the word here is the same as "transfigured" in other verses) into God's kingdom. Because of what Jesus did and by your faith, you have been brought out from under the powers of darkness that dominate the world. You have been brought under the influence and into the protection of the kingdom of love and light.

Colossians 1:14 *In whom we have redemption through his blood, [even] the forgiveness of sins.*

When man had no remedy for his sins, Jesus came and mediated a covenant between the sinner and God. The terms of this covenant made the blood of Jesus the satisfaction of the Father's justice for the sins of man. When the Father sees your faith in the shed blood of Jesus, He causes you to experience that blood as the remedy for the curse of past sins. You cannot bring your good works to God as a remedy for sin. The terms set by the mediator were His shed blood; that is the agreement the Father honors. Faith in Christ's shed blood releases you and brings you deliverance from all guilt and shame for the past. Forgiveness is a free gift in response to your faith in what Jesus has done for you on the cross.

Colossians 1:20 *And, having made peace through the blood of his cross, by him to reconcile all things unto himself; by him, [I say], whether [they be] things in earth, or things in heaven.*

Many speak of "making their peace with God." There is nothing a man or woman can do on their own to make peace with God. Where our sins are concerned, only what Jesus did on the cross will satisfy the

Father's sense of justice.

The preceding verse helps us to know how the peace of God becomes our portion and comes through the blood of Jesus. The properties of the blood are activated in your experience through your faith. The Greek word for faith in the New Testament is simply translated "confidence." Do you trust that the blood of Jesus was powerful enough to bring the peace of God into your life? Do your trust the blood of Jesus has overcome all your sinful past and purchased you a place in the family of God? If so, rest in that peace.

In God's kingdom much labor is required with many calls for service and sacrifice. However, this is where the free gift of God is brought to you by your mediator, Christ Jesus. Work was required, but Jesus did the work required for you on the cross. Jesus has brought you into friendship with God through His sacrifice, and He has brought you into a covenant with God through His blood.

Jesus has initiated you into the Kingdom by the gift of Himself on Calvary. When the situation was impossible, Jesus stepped in and gave a clear, firm path into the Father's family. Jesus is the go-between--He makes up the difference between you and the Father, and He brings you into communion with God as your Heavenly Father.

Chapter Eight: The Man Christ Jesus

1 Timothy 2:5 *For [there is] one God, and one mediator between God and men, the man Christ Jesus.*

The doctrine of Christ has three elements and are found in the verse above. (1) There is one God; (2) There is one mediator between God and man; and (3) The man Christ Jesus. Modern Christians accept that Jesus is God. However, they have problems accepting Him as a man. In the days of Jesus' earth walk, the exact opposite was true.

John 10:33 *The Jews answered him, saying, For a good work we stone thee not; but for blasphemy; and because that thou, being a man, makest thyself God.*

These Jews knew He was a man because they could see and touch Him. They watched Him as He went about His day. They knew He was a man, but they could not accept Him as God. Still, Jesus indicated He and the Father were one. When Jesus appeared to the 12 after His resurrection, Thomas knew Him for who He was in John 20:28.

John 20:28 *And Thomas answered and said unto him, My Lord and my God.*

Jesus came as a man, yet He was and is God.

John 1:1 *In the beginning was the Word, and the Word was with God, and the Word was God.*

Jesus is spoken of as the *Word of God;* the *Word is God*. God honored the Scriptures by calling Himself *the Word*. Elsewhere John calls Jesus the *Word of Life*.

John 1:14 *And the Word was made flesh, and dwelt among us, (and we beheld his glory, the glory as of the only begotten of the Father,) full of grace and truth.*

The Word is God, and Jesus is the Word made flesh, born of

Mary. Jesus is the Word--the Word is God--Jesus and the Word are one--Jesus is God. These are simple yet powerful truths. To understand that Jesus is God and He is the Word will cause you to look very reverently toward the Bible (the written Word of God). No wonder "religion" has tried to stamp these truths out and diminish the authority of the Scriptures.

Jesus is God; He is also a man. You know doubt have seen Him or let Him be God, but have you seen Him as man? Have you let Him be a man? He is the man Christ Jesus. Man (who He is); Christ (the office He fills [as Messiah]); Jesus (His mission ["Jesus" means Jehovah's salvation]). If He is not man as well as God to you, He is not Jesus because Jesus was 100 percent God and 100 percent man.

2 Corinthians 11:4 *For if he that cometh preacheth another Jesus, whom we have not preached.*

Some preach a Jesus that is only6 a man or only God. If He is not preached as man and God, you have witnessed another Jesus than the one the Apostles walked with and bore witness to in the Gospel.

Galatians 4:4 *But when the fullness of the time was come, God sent forth his Son, made of a woman, made under the law.*

Jesus did not come to earth in grandeur but in lowliness as a baby born of a woman--not in a castle but in a straw box.

Luke 2:40 *And the child grew, and waxed strong in spirit, filled with wisdom: and the grace of God was upon him.*

Jesus was not born with total wisdom and knowledge. It was necessary for him to grow physically and to develop wisdom.

Hebrews 5:8 *Though he were a Son, yet learned he obedience by the things which he suffered.*

Jesus knew the need to learn through suffering and hard experience.

Hebrew 5:7 *Who in the days of his flesh, when he had offered up prayers and supplications with strong crying and tears unto him that was able to save him from death, and was heard in that he feared.*

Jesus was driven to "strong crying and tears" as He called upon His Father for strength and protection.

John 11:35 *Jesus wept.*

Jesus knew heartache and weeping over those He loved.

John 4:6 *Now Jacob's well was there. Jesus therefore, being wearied with [his] journey, sat thus on the well: [and] it was about the sixth hour.*

Jesus grew weary and had need of rest. He did not walk around with a halo or float two feet off the ground. In order to redeem us from the curses, Jesus came to earth and became fully acquainted with the human condition before He died.

Hebrews 4:14-15 *Seeing then that we have a great high priest, that is passed into the heavens, Jesus the Son of God, let us hold fast [our] profession. (v. 15) For we have not an high priest which cannot be touched with the feeling of our infirmities; but was in all points tempted like as [we are, yet] without sin.*

The word "infirmities" here means weaknesses, frailties. There is not one aspect of mental, emotional, physical stress, or temptation that Jesus did not fully experience and endure before He went to the cross for you and me. He knows what you are going through. Remember, whatever you face He suffered before you and overcame.

Romans 8:11-12 *But if the Spirit of him that raised up Jesus from the dead dwell in you, he that raised up Christ from the dead shall also quicken your mortal bodies by his Spirit that dwelleth in you. (v. 12) Therefore, brethren, we are debtors, not to the flesh, to live after the flesh.*

If you have received Jesus as your Lord and Savior, He has taken residence in you by the same Spirit that raised Him from the dead. This Spirit not only strengthens your spirit and soul but also holds a promise of physical health and strength. You are no longer obligated to live a life ruled by the flesh (worldly, sinful tendencies) because the same Spirit dwells in you that raised Christ from the dead. Through the Spirit of God in you, it becomes possible to break the power of sin and live a holy life.

Romans 8:13 *For if ye live after the flesh, ye shall die: but if ye through the Spirit do mortify the deeds of the body, ye shall live.*

The deeds (activities) of the flesh (sinful tendencies) can be mortified (deadened, deprived of power) through the Spirit. Sin is overcome through the action of the Spirit of God in you and not just through your will power. Your will is involved, but the "power of deliverance" comes from the Spirit of Christ. Jesus limited Himself to this same Spirit in His earth walk while maintaining a sinless life.

Romans 8:14 *For as many as are led by the Spirit of God, they are the sons of God.*

Jesus (as a man) was filled and flooded with the measureless Spirit of God. He limited Himself to the resource of the Holy Spirit and did not use any secret power He did not intend to make available to you and me. All the powers He exercised on the earth were made available to us when He died and rose again.

Luke 10:19 *Behold, I give unto you power to tread on serpents and scorpions, and over all the power of the enemy: and nothing shall by any means hurt you.*

Jesus has given His power to us.

John 14:12 *Verily, verily, I say unto you, he that believeth on me, the works that I do shall he do also; and greater [works] than these shall he do; because I go unto my Father.*

Before God wraps up His eternal plan for man, there will be a people on the earth who will not only do what Jesus did in His earth walk but will go beyond these works and do greater works than He did. This boggles the mind, but the words are His, and His faith will see it happen. As a man, Jesus proved it could be done by the same Spirit He made available to you and me.

This Spirit is in you as a believer. If you say, "I accept Jesus as my Lord and Savior--He is the Lord of my life," then the seed of this power is in you. Give yourself time, and the seed of the life of God will grow in you, and you will see His power and His glory made known in your everyday life.

Chapter Nine: The Believer and the Holy Spirit

John 16:7 *Nevertheless I tell you the truth; It is expedient for you that I go away: for if I go not away, the Comforter will not come unto you; but if I depart, I will send him unto you.*

This verse contains one of the many truly astounding statements said by Jesus while He walked the earth. He said, *"It is expedient for you that I go away [for] the Comforter will not come . . ."* Let us look at the word "expedient"; it comes from the Greek word "sumphero." It is translated in other locations as profitable, better, good. It also means to contribute in order to help or profit.

The idea Jesus is conveying here is that His followers would be "better off" and more greatly profited by the Comforter He would send after His ascension. Jesus seems to say this benefit is even greater than having Him physically among them. He is saying, "You will be better off with the indwelling Comforter, the Holy Ghost, living in you than to have My very physical presence among you." The Comforter (the Holy Ghost that Jesus sent us) is the means by which He lives in the hearts of those who accept Him as Lord and Savior.

The word "Comforter" is the Greek word "parakletos." The mission the Holy Spirit fulfills by taking up residence in your heart is seen in the definition of this word. Let us define 'Comforter' further.

1. One who is called to aid of another.

The Comforter comes to live in your heart in order to aid you in every area of life. He reveals to you the knowledge of Jesus that Peter spoke of in the following verse as providing "all things that pertain to life and godliness."

2 Peter 1:3 *According as his divine power hath given unto us all things that pertain unto life and godliness, through the knowledge of him that hath called us to glory and virtue.*

2. One who pleads another's cause before a judge, a pleader,

counsel for defense, or legal assistant--an advocate.

The Holy Spirit pleads your case in prayer, inspiring you to prayer in ways you do not understand but, nonetheless, are effective in obtaining an answer from the Father.

Romans 8:26 *Likewise the Spirit also helpeth our infirmities: for we know not what we should pray for as we ought: but the Spirit itself maketh intercession for us with groanings which cannot be uttered.*

3. One who pleads another's cause, an intercessor. Christ, in His exaltation at God's right hand, pleads with God the Father for the pardon of our sins.

The Paraclete is the manifestation of God dwelling in your life, taking your needs and petitions before the throne room of God. This need for an intercessor or an advocate is somewhat behind the teaching of the Catholic Church regarding the veneration of the saints. But looking beyond the saints that have gone on before, you can see God has committed an aspect of His Person, a full third of His Being, to fulfilling just this role of personal intercession and petitioner for the affairs of the believer’s life. In view of the Father and the Son's total commitment to this role of intercessor, it is expected that reliance upon the Holy Spirit, who is praying to the Father in the name of Jesus, is the only sure certification of answered prayer according to the Scriptures.

4. The Comforter is a succorer (helper, aider, assistant). The Holy Spirit takes the place of the physical presence of Christ. He leads you to a deeper knowledge of the Gospel truth and gives you divine strength to undergo trials and persecutions on behalf of the kingdom of God.

The Holy Spirit is in residence in your life not only to provide an advocate in prayer toward heaven but to be a source of refreshing and strength in everyday life, particularly in times of great stress and suffering. He is also known as Teacher, leading believers to a more full knowledge of the Scriptures and the Christian faith. He functions as “the anointing” on teachers, pastors, and ministers in every Christian meeting. He is also the anointing on the ears of those who listen to

Gospel teaching. The Holy Spirit will give a ring of truth and conviction to a teaching as it is given. The Bible affirms this statement when it says, *"You shall know the truth and the truth will set you free."*

Luke 24:32 *And they said one to another, Did not our heart burn within us, while he talked with us by the way, and while he opened to us the scriptures?*

The teaching ministry of the Holy Spirit covers three basic areas as revealed in the following passage.

John 16:8-11 *And when he is come, he will reprove the world of sin, and of righteousness, and of judgment: (v. 9) Of sin, because they believe not on me; (v. 10) Of righteousness, because I go to my Father, and ye see me no more; (v. 11) Of judgment, because the prince of this world is judged.*

These verses speak of the Holy Spirit "reproving" the world. The word reprove is translated as "conviction" in other versions of the New Testament. The term conviction is a familiar term in Christian circles, and it carries a simple meaning. A person speaking of his convictions is speaking of truths that have been communicated deeply within his person. This conviction provokes him to actions that apply this truth to his life no matter what the cost. This conviction is a supernatural assurance which comes from the indwelling Holy Spirit that can cause you to stand and believe in faith for deliverance from the most severe trials of life.

Chapter Ten: Conviction of Sin

Jesus' estimation of the benefits of the Holy Spirit in the believer's life challenges the heart, and in this chapter we will look at the Holy Spirit's conviction in the believer's heart concerning sin.

John 16:7-8 *"It is expedient for you that I go away: for if I go not away, the Comforter will not come unto you, (v. 8) And when he is come, he will reprove the world of sin, and of righteousness, and of judgment."*

In effect Jesus is saying you are better off with His Holy Spirit living in you than if you were to have His physical presence with you. When he comes into your life, the Comforter will fulfill a three-part mission.

John 16:9 *[The Comforter will convict] of sin, because they believe not on me.*

The word "sin" was seen in a previous lesson and comes from a word meaning "to miss the mark." The preceding verse indicates that sin is a result of one who *believes not*. Sin is seen by many as a violation of any number of laws or commandments of God, and all these transgressions spring from a root problem of unbelief. If we believed in Jesus and were intimate with Him, we would not seek to meet needs in sinful ways. Christ would fill our hearts to the degree that the motivation to sin would be weakened by the motivation to have a life filled with His peace.

John the Baptist spoke of laying the "ax of truth" as the root of man's problem. Man's root problem is unbelief. Every man suffers and is guilty of this sin. Many times men commit to great works of sacrifice for God, but their motivation is they are working to be acceptable to God because they do not believe Christ did enough. Men should sacrifice and obey out of love and not unbelief. Through this error men look outwardly clean but are inwardly profane and vile.

Romans 4:8 *Blessed [is] the man to whom the Lord will not impute sin.*

The Holy Spirit living in your heart will work to communicate to you the forgiveness of God. He will strive through the Word and through the experience of God's presence to convince you that there is a place in God you may enter where sin is not counted against you.

Romans 5:19 *For as by one man's disobedience many were made sinners, so by the obedience of one shall many be made righteous.*

All men born in the human race are “born of Adam” and are considered sinners because of Adam's sin in the garden. Likewise, (in the reverse) true Christians are “born of Christ.” All those born of Christ are righteous because of Jesus obedience on the cross. God looked upon Adam's sin in the garden and saw that every man born of Adam would be guilty by birth. Then, God looked upon Jesus' obedience on the cross and was satisfied that this obedience counted for all men who would accept His Son and be born of the Spirit.

Romans 6:11 *Likewise reckon ye also yourselves to be dead indeed unto sin, but alive unto God through Jesus Christ our Lord.*

The Holy Spirit lives in you to encourage you to agree with what God says about sin in His Word. The word “reckon” in the above verse means to consider or take into account. God wants you to consider your life and that you are dead to sin. This death is not based on your effort but on the effort of Christ on the cross. If you release your faith in the cross, you will find deliverance from the sin that affects your life.

Romans 6:12 *Let not sin therefore reign in your mortal body, that ye should obey it in the lusts thereof.*

The Holy Spirit in you will provoke you to see sin as something to be abandoned and not repeated. The cycle of sin and forgiveness should not be repeated over and over in regard to the same offense. There will come a time when you should expect to overcome the sins that are besetting you now. There may be new temptations ahead, but the Bible clearly teaches that sin is not just forgiven by God but is removed from the believer's life by grace. It is not acceptable to live with repeated sin for years. Grace should be sought for deliverance.

Romans 6:14 *For sin shall not have dominion over you: for ye are not under the law, but under grace.*

The Holy Spirit delivers you from sin by influencing you and empowering you to overcome temptation. He does not deliver you by laying out new and different commands or requirements. As a believer, you do not live under a law or written requirement; you live under grace, the empowering presence of God in your life will cause you to obey without having a law to tell you right from wrong.

James 4:17 *Therefore to him that knoweth to do good, and doeth [it] not, to him it is sin.*

When we ignore the inward influence of the Holy Spirit provoking us to obey the will of God, we are in deliberate rebellion. The Holy Spirit within us becomes grieved, and the Lord seems far away. We expose ourselves to the devil and his activity in our lives by disobedience. However, by responding positively to the Holy Spirit and receiving His commands written on our hearts, we place ourselves in God's protection and will be, at times, insulated from the consequences of our own mistakes. This is the essence of God's mercy and an understanding of the indwelling Spirit's work of conviction of sin.

Chapter Eleven: Conviction of Righteousness

John 16:7 *Nevertheless I tell you the truth; It is expedient for you that I go away: for if I go not away, the Comforter will not come unto you; but if I depart, I will send him unto you.*

In this verse Jesus is "telling us the truth." The fact that He emphasizes this is an indication that He knows what He says is hard to believe. The believer is more greatly benefited by the indwelling Spirit of God that Jesus sent to the earth than He would be by the literal physical presence of Jesus walking among us.

John 16:8 *And when he is come, he will reprove the world of sin, and of righteousness, and of judgment.*

There are three basic convictions that are the work of the indwelling of the Holy Spirit:

1. Conviction of sin
2. Conviction of righteousness
3. Conviction of judgment

There is comfort from God in men's hearts when these three basic convictions are at work in them. All grief, fear, and emotional torment lead undoubtedly back to a weakening of Biblical conviction regarding Jesus' teaching in these three areas.

Righteousness

John 16:10 *Of righteousness, because I go to my Father, and ye see me no more.*

Having looked at the Holy Spirit's conviction of sin, we turn to conviction concerning righteousness. Righteousness means "right-standing." To be right with God is to have access to God. Righteousness is a sense of intimacy and agreement with the Father. Righteousness is the experience of oneness with God. The indwelling of the Holy Spirit is the medium by which God communicates this oneness to the hearts of His children.

Consider the family unit to illustrate righteousness. My children are righteous before me. They have rights to be fed, clothed, loved, and raised in my name, the Walden name. This righteousness is theirs by birth and is not something they earn. When we are born of God by believing in our heart in the resurrection of Christ and confessing Him openly as the controller of our lives, we are then born into the Father's house. As God's children, you have certain rights: Rights to pray and be heard, rights to be disciplined and trained by the Father, and rights to the protection and provision of the family name, the name of Jesus. This righteousness touches every area of life, both now and in eternity.

John 14:1-2 *Let not your heart be troubled: ye believe in God, believe also in me. (v. 2) In my Father's house are many mansions: if [it were] not [so], I would have told you. I go to prepare a place for you.*

Our place in the Father's family was personally prepared for us by Jesus. The word "mansion" here means "a dwelling place" in the original language.

John 14:3 *And if I go and prepare a place for you, I will come again, and receive you unto myself; that where I am, [there] ye may be also.*

Jesus will one day physically come again to rule the earth. But this verse also indicates that Jesus came to us in the person of the Holy Spirit to receive us into the family of God. Jesus and the Holy Spirit are one. To have the Spirit in us is to have Jesus in us. Our place in the Father's family is with Jesus. He is the elder brother, and we are the many children. He said in one place that He is not ashamed to call us brothers and sisters.

Romans 8:16-17 *The Spirit itself beareth witness with our spirit, that we are the children of God: (v. 17) And if children, then heirs; heirs of God, and joint-heirs with Christ; if so be that we suffer with [him], that we* *may be also glorified together.*

The previous verse speaks of the Holy Spirit affirming to us that we are children of God. And if we are children of God, then we are heirs, even joint heirs, with Christ. You and Jesus have the same inheritance. Jesus inherited the throne of heaven. John says in Revelation that we will reign with Jesus as kings and priests unto God.

Galatians 3:29 *And if ye [be] Christ's, then are ye Abraham's seed, and heirs according to the promise.*

Because the Holy Spirit dwells in us, we belong to Christ Jesus. And because we are the property of Jesus, we qualify for God's blessing. Blessing, therefore, is not based on works but on birth--birth into the family of God by Christ Jesus. God wants to bless who we are as well as what we do.

Titus 3:7 *That being justified by his grace, we should be made heirs according to the hope of eternal life.*

The Holy Spirit in us has made us heirs of God. It is not something we must live up to--it is ours by birth! Inheritance is a matter of birth and not works. Works should be our response of love because of the inheritance and not our attempts to earn the inheritance. The Holy Spirit will continually convict of the righteousness of God. He will continually expose to you the futility of trying to be good enough for God. God accepts you because of who Jesus is and what He has done on the cross. You do not have to earn His love. Your works and labor should be a response to the love you already are assured of having received.

Chapter Twelve: Judgment of Satan

John 16:7 *Nevertheless I tell you the truth; It is expedient for you that I go away: for if I go not away, the Comforter will not come unto you; but if I depart, I will send him unto you.*

Jesus went away via the cross. He spilled His blood in order to make a way for the Holy Spirit to take up residence in your heart. Living in your heart, the Holy Spirit pursues a threefold agenda.

John 16:8 *And when he is come, he will reprove the world of sin, and of righteousness, and of judgment.*

The subjects of sin and righteousness have been covered in the two previous lessons. Now, let us see how the Holy Spirit seeks to convince us of this judgment.

John 16:11 *Of judgment, because the prince of this world is judged.*

The prince of the world Jesus refers to here is the devil, who holds a limited power in the earth because of Adam's sin. The Holy Spirit within will continually affirm to you that the devils 's work was condemned by Jesus upon the cross. The Holy Spirit will illuminate the Word of God to you and cause you to understand and truly see that Satan is a defeated, weak, ineffective opponent of the throne of God. If you are in the God that lives on the throne and He is in you through the indwelling of the Holy Spirit, then you are made a partaker of God's dominion over Satan. Consider the following verse.

Matthew 12:29 *Or else how can one enter into a strong man's house, and spoil his goods, except he first bind the strong man? and then he will spoil his house.*

Jesus is speaking here of demonic powers that afflict men. Jesus came into the earth to bind the strength of evil. He came to stop Satan and to "spoil his house." When Adam caved in to Satan's temptation, he abdicated his God-given rights to the earth. Because of Adam's failure the whole earth became Satan's "house." In effect, Adam leased the earth that God put under his stewardship to Satan, but God held the first option to buy. When Jesus came, it was God in Christ who "entered the strong man's house," and during the three years of His earthly ministry, Jesus "spoiled his house." At the cross Jesus paid the sin-debt in full and canceled Satan's lease on the earth.

Luke 10:18 *And he said unto them, I beheld Satan as lightning fall from heaven.*

Satan operates in a spiritual dimension known as "heaven." This spiritual realm is a creation of God intended originally as the power base from which Adam would superintend the affairs of the earth. When Adam fell, Satan appropriated this throne of power and stamped all creation with his image. Jesus came and lived as a perfect man thereby invalidating Satan's legal access to what Adam put in his control four thousand years before. Paul described Jesus as the "last Adam" and the "second Man" (I Corinthians 15:45). Jesus reappropriated for man the dominion Adam gave to Satan as a consequence of his disobedience. At that moment (when Jesus came to earth), a man named Jesus was seated on the throne from which Satan had perverted God's creation for four thousand years.

Luke 11:22 *But when a stronger than he shall come upon him, and overcome him, he taketh from him all his armor wherein he trusted, and divideth his spoils.*

The restoration of human dominion on the earth is one of the spoils of Jesus' victory on the cross. Most people mistakenly view the "kingdom of God" and the "domain of darkness" as equal yet opposite powers. Understand that the domain of darkness is not equal to the kingdom of God. Satan is a created, limited, and finite being. He has a beginning and an ending. His powers are limited. God in us is infinite, and His kingdom is unlimited. Satan's kingdom is bounded by the kingdom of God on every side. If you were to traverse the domain of darkness from pole to pole, you would find the kingdom of God at either boundary.

John 12:31 *Now is the judgment of this world: now shall the prince of this world be cast out.*

Satan's limited power was destroyed over the lives of men after the cross. Men continue to be tormented by Satan because of ignorance and rejection of God's plan of restoration through Christ. When man rebels against God, his only option is submission to the domain of darkness. This is because man was not created as an independent entity. Man is an image-bearer. He will bear the image of one spiritual being or the other--either God or the devil. Man is a mirror; God is light. If there is no light, he is in darkness, and Satan is the prince of darkness. The man that accepts Christ as Savior receives light and can live above the influence of the domain of darkness.

Hebrews 2:14 *Forasmuch then as the children are partakers of flesh and blood, he also himself likewise took part of the same; that through death he might destroy him that had the power of death, that is, the devil.*

Jesus defeated the devil on his own ground. The devil gained control over all flesh because of Adam's disobedience, but Jesus came born of flesh and blood and overcame Satan in his own realm of authority. With the handicap of being a man, Jesus competed with Satan. He did not use any ability to overcome Satan that He did not intend to make available to the believer through the shedding of His blood. As flesh and blood, Jesus limited himself to exercising only that power that He planned to make available to you and me. As a born-again believer conducting your life in the same context that Jesus conducted His, you will experience the same results He did. You do not have to accept the peril and heartache the devil throws your way. By faith in the blood of Christ and bold prayers of hope, you can overcome.

John 5:19 *Then answered Jesus and said unto them, Verily, verily, I say* *unto you, The Son can do nothing of himself, but what he seeth the Father do: for what things soever he doeth, these also doeth the Son likewise.*

John 5:30 *I can of mine own self do nothing: as I hear, I judge: and my judgment is just; because I seek not mine own will, but the will of the Father which hath sent me.*

There will come a time after Jesus sets up His kingdom as a physical power on the earth that Satan will be permanently removed from the earth.

Revelation 20:10 *And the that deceived them was cast into the lake of fire and brimstone, where the beast and the false prophet [are], and shall be tormented day and night forever and ever.*

In the meantime he is an adversary that we are well-equipped in the name of Jesus to overcome.

Ephesians 6:12 *For we wrestle not against flesh and blood, but against principalities, against powers, against the rulers of the darkness of this world, against spiritual wickedness in high [places].*

In this life never be mislead into seeing your struggles as being primarily physical, financial, or relational. People are not the problem. Poverty is not the problem. The problem is an unseen enemy trying to gain ground over you that Jesus died to gain on your behalf. You can rise up in prayer and faith and verbally forbid the enemy from touching your life. God has put the backing of His kingdom behind your prayer of faith.

The Holy Spirit within will consistently affirm in you that "greater is He that is in you than he that is in the world." Who will you believe--the author of your bad circumstance or the author of your salvation? Be bold, and stand against the enemy's lies. You will find all heaven backing your prayers, and miracles will begin to happen.

Chapter Thirteen: Foundational Doctrines

In the letter to the Hebrews, Paul attempted to address the Jewish church concerning some deep truths in the Word of God. In the fifth chapter he makes this statement:

Hebrews 5:11-12 *[Now] Concerning [Jesus our High Priest] we have much to say which is hard to explain, since you have become dull in your [spiritual] hearing and sluggish, even slothful [in achieving spiritual insight]. (v. 12) For even though by this time you ought to be teaching others, you actually need someone to teach you over again the very first principles of God's Word [i.e. the doctrine of Christ]. You have come to need milk not solid food.* Amplified Bible

Paul's indication here is that the average believer should be a teacher of God's truth, not just the pastor. He says to us all, "You ought to be teachers." Being educated in the first principles of the faith, you should then accept the role of teaching others what you have learned.

In previous lessons you learned that the doctrine of Christ is the doctrine or teaching concerning whom Jesus is, His mission, and His message. The Scripture that most clearly states the doctrine of Christ is I Timothy 2:5.

I Timothy 2:5 *For [there is] one God, and one mediator between God and men, the man Christ Jesus;*

In this study we find that Paul is expanding on the doctrine of Christ. Having taught the doctrine of Christ, He goes on to point out that there are principles of truth based on that doctrine. These doctrines are principles, understandings, and applications of the doctrine of Christ for everyday living.

The Greek word for "principle" here is defined as the "elements of a thing," the "letters of the alphabet," or the "ABCs" of the faith. In other words, there are teachings associated with the doctrine of Christ that are considered the ABCs of the Christian faith. There are six of them listed in Hebrews 6:1-3. The Hebrews knew these ABCs of the faith, and now they and we are called upon by the Apostle Paul to move on to maturity.

Hebrews 6:1-3 *Therefore leaving the principles of the doctrine of Christ, let us go on unto perfection; not laying again the foundation of repentance from dead works, and of faith toward God, (v. 2) Of the doctrine of baptisms, and of laying on of hands, and of resurrection of the dead, and of eternal judgment. (v. 3) And this will we do, if God permit.*

Here are six foundational principles or ABCs of Christian doctrine. These are things you should be familiar with and be able to teach others. It is important not to just look at these teachings as separate, unrelated doctrines of the Bible. Together and individually they are known as principles of ABCs of the doctrine of Christ that we studied earlier.

1. The Foundation of Repentance From Dead Works
2. The Foundation of Faith Toward God
3. The Foundation of the Doctrine of Baptisms
4. The Foundation of Laying on of Hands
5. The Foundation of Resurrection From the Dead
6. The Foundation of Eternal Judgment

ABCs are part of the alphabet. The alphabet gives a linguistic breakdown of our English. What the alphabet is to the English language, these teachings are to the doctrine of Christ. These six teachings show how the doctrine of Christ breaks down and is applied to human life. These teachings say to us: "Because of who Jesus is and what He has done, this (teaching or doctrine) is true in the world and in the individual life of the one who believes in Jesus Christ."

These six teachings show you how to act on the doctrine of

Christ. In effect, "Because of who Jesus is, I believe this, I practice this, and I expect this to happen . . ." With this in mind let us continue the study of these elements or ABCs of the doctrine of Christ.

Chapter Fourteen: Repentance from Dead Works

There are six teachings listed in Hebrews 6:1-2 that cover the basic applications of the doctrine of Christ to the believer's life. They represent the rudiments of Bible teaching that the Apostle Paul considered the base line of all Christian instruction. Everyone should know and be able to teach others these things. These teachings are not simply intellectual facts; they are universal applications of the doctrine of Christ in the believer's life and experience. They are how the believer becomes a "doer of the Word" with respect to I Timothy 2:5, *"There [is only] one God, and [only] one mediator between God and men, the Man Christ Jesus."* In other words, because of who Jesus is, these six teachings are a reality in the individual believer's life and in the world. This lesson covers the application of repentance from dead works.

Hebrews 6:1 *Therefore leaving the principles of the doctrine of Christ, let us go on unto perfection; not laying again the foundation of repentance from dead works.*

Not surprisingly, repentance is the first on the list of things that men are called to learn about walking with Jesus. The Greek word for "repentance" here is "metanoia." It is used 24 times in the New Testament and is defined as, "a change of mind: as it appears to one who repents of a purpose he has formed or of something he has done."

Another Greek lexicon defines this "repentance" as "to abandon evil." As an application of the doctrine of Christ, this foundation means that you repent and abandon evil or ungodly practices because you are now associated with Christ. What passed for an acceptable lifestyle before you came to Christ is not acceptable now (others may, you cannot). Maybe others can do such and such, but you cannot do these things because now you belong to Christ, and your life is His to command.

I Corinthians 6:20 *For ye are bought with a price: therefore glorify God in your body, and in your spirit, which are God's.*

This repentance is uniquely "Christian" repentance. Only Christians have the grace from God to "abandon evil." A non-Christian may try and amend his ways, but until the blood of Christ is applied to his heart, the corruption will surface again and again.

Jeremiah 17:9 *The heart [is] deceitful above all [things], and desperately wicked: who can know it?*

As a Christian, you are now empowered to overcome the sin-force in your life by the grace and influence provided to you when Jesus died on the cross. You are not only forgiven, but you are empowered by Jesus' death on the cross to overcome sin and live above it. This is not something you do in yourself, but it is something that the indwelling Comforter is at work in you to accomplish. Your place is to acknowledge Him and cooperate with Him as He cleanses you from all the impurities of life.

I John 1:5 *This then is the message which we have heard of him, and declare unto you, that God is light, and in him is no darkness at all.*

The verse above says, "God is light." If you are born of God, this light is in you, and you are in it. He is the Comforter who is come to teach you and empower you in life. He enables you to walk in this light. Thus, He empowers you to go out and be Jesus to the world.

I John 1:7 *But if we walk in the light, as he is in the light, we have fellowship one with another, and the blood of Jesus Christ his Son cleanseth us from all sin.*

The blood of Jesus not only brings forgiveness of past sin, but it diminishes (through grace) your vulnerability to sin. Be very clear on this point. A Christian is not as vulnerable to sin and sinfulness as the non-Christian. This is not something he does within himself; rather, it is a result of the indwelling Spirit. It is nothing to boast about as though it were an accomplishment of your own. It is a work of grace.

I John 1:8 *If we say that we have no sin, we deceive ourselves, and the truth is not in us.*

Left alone, you would inevitably fall. The fact is, however, that you are not left to yourself. The empowering presence of God is within you offering you victory over all impurity and uncleanness.

I John 3:9 *Whosoever is born of God doth not commit sin; for his seed remaineth in him: and he cannot sin, because he is born of God.*

If you have accepted Jesus from the heart as your Savior, you are born of God. Being born of God, the seed of God is in you. In the book of Galatians, Paul reveals this "seed" as the person of Jesus (himself) living in the heart of the believer.

Galatians 3:16 *Now to Abraham and his seed were the promises made. He saith not, And to seeds, as of many; but as of one, And to thy seed, which is Christ.*

I Peter 1:23 *Being born again, not of corruptible seed, but of incorruptible, by the word of God, which liveth and abideth for ever.*

This is a great mystery. The seed of God is in you. This seed is a manifestation of God (himself) dwelling in your heart, and the part of God that is in you cannot sin. If you are born of God (and you are), that part of you is made free from the obligation of the Adamic nature to sin. Look at the following verse.

I John 3:6 *Whosoever abideth in him sinneth not: whosoever sinneth hath not seen him, neither known him.*

The word "abide" means to "remain, continue, endure, not to depart, to wait for (Christ), to remain as one." In short, if your heart is stayed on Christ and not looking right or left at the temptations of the world, then you will become free from any and all evil and sin in your life that may plague you from time to time. The Christian life is not just an endless cycle of sinning and being forgiven. The Word of God holds promises to deliver us from the chains of sinfulness and wickedness.

I John 5:18 *We know that whosoever is born of God sinneth not; but he that is begotten of God keepeth himself, and that wicked one toucheth him not.*

The above verse is a key. According to the Word of God, you can be "untouchable" if you are born of God. You can experience a place in God where "the wicked one" touches you not! This is not some special privilege for only a few "holy ones." This is a benefit that Jesus died to deliver to you and me as average believers. Isaiah said Jesus was "bruised for our iniquities." The word "iniquity" in the Old Testament means "lawlessness." He died to forgive all mankind and also to deliver man from the lawlessness of His ancient progenitor and father, Adam. Jesus died to deliver man from the satanic influence that Adam introduced into the human race through his disobedience.

Romans 6:6 *Knowing this, that our old man is crucified with [him], that the body of sin might be destroyed, that henceforth we should not serve sin.*

The term "old man" in the New Testament refers to the aspect of our person that would lead us in wickedness and sin. As far a God is concerned, your "old man" died on the cross, and when you become a believer in Jesus, you can then enter into the experience of that reality. You do not have to serve sin and Satan. You can now serve as God's Son.

Romans 8:12 *Therefore, brethren, we are debtors, not to the flesh, to live after the flesh.*

Because of Jesus' work on the cross, you are no longer indebted or obligated to sin. We often hear men say, "I could not help myself . . ." In the unbeliever sin is "standard equipment,"and in the "new creation" it is optional. You are not obligated to sin a little every day. Through your intimacy with Christ, God helps you and gives you power to obey and overcome the most severe temptations.

Chapter Fifteen: Faith Toward God

We are covering the six teachings listed in Hebrews 6:1 and 2 which teach the basic applications of the doctrine of Christ. They represent the rudiments of Bible teaching that the Apostle Paul considered the base line of all Christian instruction. Each one of us should know and be able to teach others these things since these teachings reveal the "doing" of I Timothy 2:5, *"That there [is only] one God, and [only] one mediator between God and men, the Man Christ Jesus."* Because of who Jesus is, these six teachings are a reality in the individual believer's life and in the world. Let us go to the second teaching.

Hebrews 6:1 *Therefore leaving the principles of the doctrine of Christ, let us go on unto perfection; not laying again the foundation of repentance from dead works, and of faith toward God.*

The word "repent" here means to "abandon evil." This is Christian repentance. In the Gospels where John the Baptist preaches repentance, the original word means "to hate evil." The difference is that John's message speaks to those who do not know Christ. These people are incapable of abandoning evil ways because Christ has not come into their heart. Once you become a Christian and Christ enters your heart, you are then empowered not just to hate sin but to overcome it by means of faith toward God.

The word "faith" in the New Testament very simply means "confidence." In Hebrews the writer qualifies faith as being "toward God." Everyone in the earth has faith in something or toward something be it science, religion, Buddha, Mohammed, or whatever. Everyone has faith. When you are born again and Christ enters your heart, you begin to develop faith toward God. In simple terms faith is a state of trust and peace in the heart. This trust or confidence is a natural response to having a personal encounter with the Lord Jesus Christ. You know beyond a shadow of doubt that He loves you, has given His life for you, and that He sits on the throne of the universe as your intercessor and friend. This faith is what Jesus said He would be looking for when He returns to earth.

Luke 18:8 *When the Son of man cometh, shall he find faith on the earth?*

What an amazing statement. Jesus is saying that on His return He is not going to take inventory of all the church buildings we have built nor is He going to review all the missions or soup kitchens we have sponsored. Here is the heart cry of the Heavenly Father. When He sends His Son to establish His reign in the earth as a physical kingdom, will He find people who are living in simple trust in him? That is what will satisfy His heart as opposed to all the grandiose things men supposedly do to His glory.

Hebrews 11:6 *But without faith [it is] impossible to please [him]: for he that cometh to God must believe that he is, and [that] he is a rewarder of them that diligently seek him.*

Do you desire to please the Lord? Then seek to do so by childlike faith. It is impossible to please the Father any other way. He is not influenced by our sacrifice, diligence, religious observance, or suffering unless these things are born of childlike faith. These things are no pleasure to the Father unless they have been initiated in a heart of simple trust in Him.

Faith has two components. First, faith requires a belief that "God is." Most men believe in the existence of God, but this verse (Heb. 11:6) is speaking of specific belief in Him as He has revealed Himself to us. Here is a list of the names for God from the Bible that tells us how God himself wants us to see Him.

- El-Shaddai [All Sufficient One]
- Jehovah-Jireh [Our Provider]

- Jehovah-Nissi [Our Standard]
- Jehovah-Rophi [Our Healer]
- Jehovah-Shalom [Our Peace]
- Jehovah-Shammah [God is Near]
- Jehovah-Tsidkenu [Our Righteousness]

Faith that believes "God is" believes that He will be who He has revealed himself to be. When you are sick, He is Jehovah-rophi, the God who heals you; when you are in financial need, He is Jehovah-Jireh, the God who provides for you; and when you are troubled, He is Jehovah-Shalom, the God who is peace in the midst of the storm.

Faith's second component is to believe He is the rewarder of them that diligently seek Him. The first component of faith addresses your attitude (i.e., you believe that He is the answer to your need). The second component addresses your actions (i.e., because of who God is, you will live in trust toward Him, expecting Him to be faithful to the promises of His Word).

The Greek word "diligence" in this verse implies that you would "seek after the Lord, to investigate thoroughly the Lord's promise." The root word means: "To seek in order to find out by thinking, meditating, reasoning out the promises of God; to inquire into the promises of God; to seek after God, seek for His blessing, aim at the Lord, strive after the Lord; to seek Him, require, demand; to crave, demand something from someone."

It seems the Lord is saying to us that He does not want us to take no for an answer. He does not want us to allow ourselves to be talked out of His goodness. He is willing to reward us, but there are many out there that will tell you God does not care about you or your health or your daily needs. Yet, He instructed us to pray that He would give us daily bread!

Hebrews 11:3 *Through faith we understand that the worlds were framed by the word of God, so that things which are seen were not* *made of things which do appear.*

Where did God get the power to create the universe? This verse reveals the secret. Faith was the secret power of God's creative ability. He formed the worlds by faith, and your world or your life is formed by faith also. The form or manner of your life has been shaped by what you have expected or had confidence would happen in your life. If you do not like the way things have shaped up in your life, then change your expectations from lack, sickness, poverty, and family problems to the promises of God. He will take your life and form it into a life that will bring glory to Him rather than suffering and heartache to you.

Hebrews 11:1 *Now faith is the substance of things hoped for, the evidence of things not seen.*

Faith substantiates or brings into reality the things that one wishes for himself or herself. You can wish for things to change and hope that they will get better, but until you direct that faith at Jesus who died to bring deliverance and salvation, nothing will ever happen. However, when you turn to Him in faith and confidence that He will deliver, save, and redeem you in every area of your life, then you will see things begin to turn around.

Chapter Sixteen: Baptisms

Hebrews 6:1-2 *Therefore leaving the principles of the doctrine of Christ, let us go on unto perfection; not laying again the foundation of repentance from dead works, and of faith toward God,(v. 2) Of the doctrine of baptisms, and of laying on of hands, and of resurrection of the dead, and of eternal judgment.*

Each one of these teachings builds upon the one before it. If there is no repentance, faith cannot be effective. Once faith comes then the doctrine of baptisms can become a living thing rather than a vain religious observance.

In the church the Lord requires those born into His family to be baptized. In the Old Testament those who were born into the natural family of God (the Jews) were required to be circumcised. So what circumcision was to the Jews, baptism is to the Christian. Circumcision was a sign to each male child that God was in covenant with Him and that he was in covenant with God.

Likewise, baptism is a sign of a new life with Christ as opposed to the old life without God. The doctrine of baptisms is plural. Many times God came and renewed His covenant with Abraham. In the Christian life there are different times, events, and experiences whereby God will reaffirm and expand His covenant of life and blessing with the child of God.

There are basically three aspects of baptism spoken of in the New Testament.

Matthew 3:11 *I indeed baptize you with water unto repentance: but he that cometh after me is mightier than I, whose shoes I am not worthy to bear: he shall baptize you with the Holy Ghost, and [with] fire.*

Baptism in water should follow immediately after a person

accepts Christ as his Savior. There is much discussion about infant baptism and whether to sprinkle with water or to immerse. This should not be a point of contention. The word "baptize" comes from a Greek word meaning "to immerse." This clearly indicates something more involved than just sprinkling. Also in the New Testament, water baptism came after an adult or child understood their need of Christ as Savior and having made a conscious decision to follow the Lord Jesus Christ. However, I would not minimize infant baptism or say that if you have been sprinkled in baptism that this is not satisfactory. If you are satisfied with your baptism, then do not allow anyone to shake you. However, after infant baptism and sprinkling, I would add that immersion as an adult after receiving Christ as personal Lord and Savior would not diminish but rather enhance and underscore the spiritual meaning of infant sprinkling. Church authorities may not agree on this. Catholic authorities will object, and Protestant theologians will cry "heresy!" But the plain fact is that the church [Protestant or Catholic] will not save you, and the important issue is peace with God and satisfying His heart by full obedience to His command.

John said that Jesus would come and accompany water baptism with "baptism in the Holy Ghost." The first experience of the baptism of the Holy Ghost is recorded in Acts 2.

Acts 2:1-4 *And when the day of Pentecost was fully come, they were all with one accord in one place. (v. 2) And suddenly there came a sound from heaven as of a rushing mighty wind, and it filled all the house where they were sitting. (v. 3) And there appeared unto them cloven tongues like as of fire, and it sat upon each of them. (v. 4) And they were all filled with the Holy Ghost, and began to speak with other tongues, as the Spirit gave them utterance.*

For over two centuries after the day of Pentecost, church historians tell us it was the common experience of believers to speak and pray in heavenly languages unknown to them; however, when the shadow of the dark ages fell over medieval times, these gifts and graces diminished greatly. To explain, these theologians concluded that this gift, along with the gifts of miracles, healing, etc., had passed away and were no longer needed. Then from the mid 1800s through the early 1900s, a revival of Pentecostal experience swept the church world. (This Pentecostal experience is not to be confused with the denomination that uses this name.)

The personal experience of baptism in the Holy Spirit accompanied with praying in heavenly languages once again became a common experience in the Christian world. Great healing ministries have emerged, and thousands have witnessed the miracle-working power of God. The traditional churches have been very hesitant to acknowledge this renewal, but over time the Catholic Church, many Baptist denominations, and others have given the nod to these graces of God.

The baptism of the Holy Spirit is an experience that usually comes to believers in a season of prayer just as in the days of Acts. These men and women spent some ten days in prayer and then suddenly experienced an outward sense of God's presence in the form of a wind in the house. Today, however, many believers report this experience as a tingling or overwhelming sense of fullness in the chest which is not unpleasant. At some point an utterance of an unknown language will present itself to the person in prayer. He will feel unsatisfied to pray in his mother tongue and will take this foreign phrase on his lips in prayer. This action will generally bring a great sense of spiritual release and lightness. After this initial baptism, the believers find they can use this heavenly language at will in times of praise and thanksgiving as well as intercession for needs in their lives and the lives of others. This experience will be covered in more detail in a later lesson.

The last baptism that John spoke of was the baptism of fire. In addressing this baptism, Bible teachers in traditional churches and the "Spirit-filled" churches have made a common mistake. Churches (who did not speak with tongues) taught that when you were water baptized you received the baptism of Spirit and fire in a figure at the same time.

Churches that accept speaking with tongues believe water baptism and Holy Ghost baptism are two separate aspects of the "one baptism" taught in the New Testament, but the baptism of fire was received in a figure when one was baptized in the Holy Spirit.

The clear indication seems to be, however, that the one baptism taught in Ephesians 4:1-8 is expressed in three aspects of water, Spirit, and fire. These are different experiences distinct from one another. Baptism in water is widely practiced in the Christian world. Baptism in the Holy Ghost has also become a common experience. But the baptism in fire is something yet to become clearly known. If we have not received the baptism of fire yet, what must that be like? Remember that the New Testament speaks of Jesus as the author and finisher of our faith. Therefore, we can look at the life of Jesus to see an example of the baptism of fire.

Matthew 17:1-2, 5 *And after six days Jesus taketh Peter, James, and John his brother, and bringeth them up into an high mountain apart, (v. 2) And was transfigured before them: and his face did shine as the sun, and his raiment was white as the light. (v. 5) While he yet spake, behold, a bright cloud overshadowed them: and behold a voice out of the cloud, which said, This is my beloved Son, in whom I am well pleased; hear ye him.*

In I Corinthians the New Testament says that when He appears we shall be like Him because we shall see Him face to face. In the book of Acts when Steven was stoned, his face shone like an angel. Many times in the New Testament when the Lord or an angel appeared to men, they were in "shining apparel." In looking at the baptism in fire, I believe we need to be like the 120 before the Spirit came. They were told to wait and expect the blessing of the Lord, but they were not quite sure what it would be like in manner and form.

It is so easy to explain away and trivialize the promises of God, particularly if we have not experienced them because no flesh wants to admit that there is something in God we have not attained. Paul said he did not consider himself having attained but that he was pressing on. So, we cannot speak clearly about the baptism in fire as to what it is, but we can speak boldly about what it is not--it is not something to be explained away by the religious crowd but is something to ponder and to say within ourselves that God has greater things in store for His people than have yet been revealed.

Chapter Seventeen: Laying on of Hands

We continue the six teachings listed in Hebrews 6:1-2 that cover the basic applications of the doctrine of Christ. We have covered repentance, faith, and baptisms. These three deal with our response to the reality of who is Jesus. The final three teachings involve His response to our faith. The first three teachings deal with obedience; the last three teachings address the blessings of God on the obedient. They touch on the impartation of God's power into our lives and His posture toward us in regard to eternity.

Hebrews 6:1-2 *Therefore leaving the principles of the doctrine of Christ, let us go on unto perfection; not laying again the foundation of repentance from dead works, and of faith toward God, (v. 2) Of the doctrine of baptisms, and of laying on of hands . . .*

What is the significance of the laying on of hands? Is it merely a form or a ceremony? In Bible times the laying on of hands was viewed as a means of imparting life and blessing. Even medical science today has established the nurturing impartation of the human touch. The first instance recorded in the Bible of this practice was when Jacob laid his hands on his grandsons to bless them in Gen. 48:13-22.

Genesis 48:13, 15-16 *And Joseph took them both, Ephraim in his right hand toward Israel's left hand, and Manasseh in his left hand toward Israel's right hand, and brought [them] near unto him. (v. 15) And he blessed Joseph, and said, God, before whom my fathers Abraham and Isaac did walk, the God which fed me all my life long unto this day, (v. 16) The Angel which redeemed me from all evil, bless the lads; and let my name be named on them, and the name of my fathers Abraham and Isaac; and let them grow into a multitude in the midst of the earth.*

In Old Testament times the laying on of hands was seen as a means of imposing responsibility and obligation and also of imparting blessing. In the Old Testament the worshipers would lay their hands on the animal sacrifice, symbolically imparting or transferring guilt and blame from the worshiper to the beast. In the New Testament church, we lift our hands in worship services saying, in effect, that Jesus has transferred to Himself the weight of our sin and guilt and freed us from penalty. Lifting of hands is the act of transferring grace, burdens, or praise to God.

In the early church the laying on of hands was understood to be a channel of spiritual transmission from one to another. The hands themselves are a symbol denoting service to God or ministry. The open hand (even today) is a universal symbol of service and supply of that which is lacking.

Psalms 145:16 *Thou openest thine hand, and satisfiest the desire of every living thing.*

Psalms 104:28 *[That] thou givest them they gather: thou openest thine hand, they are filled with good.*

The "hand of the Lord" is a common phrase in the Old Testament. The hand of the Lord in a situation would refer to God's judgment.

Exodus 9:3 *Behold, the hand of the LORD is upon thy cattle which [is] in the field, upon the horses, upon the asses, upon the camels, upon the oxen, and upon the sheep: [there shall be] a very grievous murrain.*

Deuteronomy 2:15 *For indeed the hand of the LORD was against them, to destroy them from among the host, until they were consumed.*

The hand also represents God's deliverance.

Exodus 13:3 *And Moses said unto the people, Remember this day, in which ye came out from Egypt, out of the house of bondage; for by strength of hand the LORD brought you out from this [place] . . .*

The hand of the Lord was seen as anointing or empowering of men for service.

Ezekiel 1:3 *The word of the LORD came expressly unto Ezekiel the priest, . . . and the hand of the LORD was there upon him.*

Ezekiel 37:1 *The hand of the LORD was upon me, and carried me out in the spirit of the LORD. . .*

As you will remember, the laying on of hands and the doctrine of Christ are foundational doctrines which deal with the practical application of the doctrine of Christ in our lives. In other words, this is true or this is our experience because Christ is in us. There is in the believer the ability to receive impartation and to impart through the laying on of hands. Just as God moves through a Bible study, through prayer, and in other ways, He has blessings to release to His children through the ministry of the laying on of hands.

There are five functions of the laying on of hands in the life of the believer.

1. Impartation

There is an actual impartation to you when hands are laid on you in prayer. Science has proven that hands impart a force of energy. In the late 1960s a biochemist and enzymologist, M. Justa Smith, did extensive research on the biochemical effect of energy imparted through the laying on of hands. Her research detected the presence of a magnetic field associated with the laying on of hands.

Dr. Dolores Krieger of New York University compared blood samples of subjects subjected to the laying on of hands. Her findings showed that the laying on of hands raised the hemoglobin levels in the blood samples of people who had hands laid on them for a specific period of time. Science has, therefore, provided a supporting statistic in line with God's Word. There is an actual impartation of vitality and influence through the laying on of hands. This includes not only physical impartation but spiritual impartation as well. A new dimension of supernatural and spiritual impartation through God's power is added to your life when you have hands laid on you by a Spirit-filled believer.

2. Identification

With the laying on of hands, there is also an identification that takes place. In the Old Testament offering, there was an identification of the worshiper with the sacrificial animal he brought to the Lord. He would lay his hands on the animal, and his life would be identified with the animal's life that was then offered to God.

3. Confirmation

There is also an act of confirmation by the laying on of hands. In Acts 14:22-23 we find in practice that the Apostles would confirm the souls of the saints at the same time they would ordain the church leaders. Ordination certainly involved the laying on of hands and also, no doubt, did confirmation which served to comfort, encourage, and establish believers in the faith and in membership within the local church.

4. Ministry of Healing and Blessing

The laying on of hands implies the release of God's blessing upon one who has hands laid upon him or her by a Spirit-filled believer.

Mark 10:13, 16 *And they brought young children to him, that he should touch them . . . . (v. 16) And he took them up in his arms, put [his] hands upon them, and blessed them.*

James 5:14-15 *Is any sick among you? let him call for the elders of the church; and let them pray over him, anointing him with oil in the name of the Lord; (v. 15) And the prayer of faith shall save the sick, and the Lord shall raise him up; and if he have committed sins, they shall be forgiven him.*

There is a provision in the church of health and healing through prayer and the laying on of hands. The hand transmits what the prayer dictates. This is to be sought in times of physical suffering, and healing is expected to be the result.

5. Ordination or Commission to Christian Service

The laying on of hands was practiced as a vital part of preparing and empowering elders and deacons.

Acts 6:6 *Whom [the deacons] were set before the apostles: and when they had prayed, they laid [their] hands on them.*

I Timothy 4:14 *Neglect not the gift that is in thee, which was given thee by prophecy, with the laying on of the hands of the presbytery.*

The laying on of hands is a dynamic means by which the believer experiences the miracles of God in his life. It has been long neglected and greatly misunderstood in Christianity. But in the doctrine of Christ and its application in your everyday life, you should seek this ministry, and minister the same to others in need around you.

Chapter Eighteen: Resurrection from the Dead

This is the continuation of our study of the foundational principles of the doctrine of Christ. This lesson concerns the doctrine of the resurrection from the dead.

Hebrews 6:1-3 *Therefore leaving the principles of the doctrine of Christ, let us go on unto perfection; not laying again the foundation of repentance from dead works, and of faith toward God, (v. 2) Of the doctrine of baptisms, and of laying on of hands, and of resurrection of the dead, and of eternal judgment. (v. 3) And this will we do, if God permit.*

The word resurrection is defined in Greek as follows: *'anastasis' {an-as'-tas-is} 1) a raising up, rising (as from a seat) 2) a rising from the dead 2a) that of Christ 2b) that of all men at the end of this present age.*

The whole thought of resurrection is shrouded in mystery. Men are intrigued with the concept of eternity yet unwilling to accept the finality of judgment outside of Christ. Man is an eternal being. Every man ever born on the earth is still aware and in existence somewhere in eternity. Being made in the image of God, we are eternal beings. Every one of us (regardless of our beliefs) will spend eternity somewhere. At a certain point in God's timetable, every one of us will give an account of ourselves before Him. Paul spoke of the resurrection as something to be looked forward to and attained.

Philippians 3:10-11 *That I may know him, and the power of his resurrection, and the fellowship of his sufferings, being made conformable unto his death; (v. 11) If by any means I might attain unto the resurrection of the dead.*

The previous four topics in the doctrine of Christ dealt with this present time and what is available to man in Christ today. This fourth topic and the one following deal with eternity and man's final disposition before God. In many places the salvation of the soul is described as resurrection. According to Scripture we are indeed raised up to newness of life when we accept Christ as our Savior.

Ephesians 2:1, 5-6 *And you [hath he quickened], who were dead in trespasses and sins; (v. 5) Even when we were dead in sins, hath quickened us together with Christ, (by grace ye are saved;) (v. 6) And hath raised [us] up together, and made [us] sit together in heavenly [places] in Christ Jesus . . .*

There will also be a resurrection of the body and a reunion of departed souls to their physical remains from which they were separated by death.

John 5:25 *Verily, verily, I say unto you, The hour is coming, and now is, when the dead shall hear the voice of the Son of God: and they that hear shall live.*

Both the just and the unjust will have a part in the resurrection. To the just it shall be a resurrection of life; they shall receive a body like Christ's resurrected form.

Romans 6: 4-5 *Therefore we are buried with him by baptism into death: that like as Christ was raised up from the dead by the glory of the Father, even so we also should walk in newness of life. (v. 5) For if we have been planted together in the likeness of his death, we shall be also [in the likeness] of [his] resurrection . . .*

To the unjust the resurrection is condemnation for sinful lives and the rejection of Jesus Christ as his/her personal Savior.

II Corinthians 5:10 *For we must all appear before the judgment seat of Christ; that every one may receive the things [done] in [his] body, according to that he hath done, whether [it be] good or bad.*

Revelation 20:12 *And I saw the dead, small and great, stand before God; and the books were opened: and another book was opened, which* *is [the book] of life: and the dead were judged out of those things which were written in the books, according to their works.*

The resurrection will be at a specific time in the future, and there will be believers in Jesus alive on the earth at that time. They will receive a "glorified" body and go to heaven without having to pass through the threshold of death.

I Corinthians 15:13-19 *But if there be no resurrection of the dead, then is Christ not risen: (v. 14) And if Christ be not risen, then [is] our preaching vain, and your faith [is] also vain. (v. 15) Yea, and we are found false witnesses of God; because we have testified of God that he raised up Christ: whom he raised not up, if so be that the dead rise not. (v. 16) For if the dead rise not, then is not Christ raised: (v. 17) And if Christ be not raised, your faith [is] vain; ye are yet in your sins. (v. 18) Then they also which are fallen asleep in Christ are perished. (v. 19) If in this life only we have hope in Christ, we are of all men most miserable.*

We need to hear what Paul is saying. Here is a man who had experienced the greatest degree of God's spirit available to man in this life. He is arguably the most godly man who has ever lived and is pointing us to the great and wonderful things that God has prepared for us in eternity. Paul is saying that no matter how wonderful or gracious the Lord may be to us in this life we cannot conceive of the marvels He has in store for us in eternity.

I Corinthians 15:20-23 But now is Christ risen from the dead, [and] become the first fruits of them that slept. (v. 21) For since by man [came] death, by man [came] also the resurrection of the dead. (v. 22) For as in Adam all die, even so in Christ shall all be made alive. (v. 23) But every man in his own order: Christ the first fruits; afterward they that are Christ's at his coming.

When Jesus comes again, we who belong to Him will be raised up from this existence even as He was raised from the dead. By calling Himself the "first fruits from the dead," Jesus is indicating to us that we, too, are destined to taste of the victory He tasted when the stone rolled away from His tomb, and He came out of the grave victorious over sin and the grave.

I Corinthians 15:26 *The last enemy [that] shall be destroyed [is] death.*

God the Father sees death as an enemy of His purpose. The reality of the resurrection is an expression of the Father's hatred of death and sickness and sin. One day He will fully deal with death, hell, and the grave and put them away forever from before His people. If you belong to Him, you will take part in that blessing.

I Corinthians 15:35 *But some [man] will say, How are the dead raised up? and with what body do they come?*

Men have a hard time seeing anything other than harps and fleecy white clouds when they think of heaven. For myself that would be a hellish existence. Heaven is not going to be some simplistic place of endless inactivity. There is a plan that God will unfold before us for eternity, and we will take part in it. There will be work to do and challenges to meet. It will be a glorious family working together to please the Father's heart.

I Corinthians 15:49-52 *And as we have borne the image of the earthy, we shall also bear the image of the heavenly. (v. 50) Now this I say, brethren, that flesh and blood cannot inherit the kingdom of God; neither doth corruption inherit incorruption. (v. 51) Behold, I shew you a mystery; We shall not all sleep, but we shall all be changed, (v. 52) In a moment, in the twinkling of an eye, at the last trump: for the trumpet shall sound, and the dead shall be raised incorruptible, and we shall be changed.*

There will be no corruption inward or outward when we are resurrected. Every defect of spirit, soul, and body will be absent. There will be perfect health with no pain. There will be perfect peace and joy. There will be memory but no pain associated with it for He will wipe away every tear from our eye. As children of God, this is a glorious hope that we should look forward to and greatly anticipate as part of our inheritance.

Chapter Nineteen: Eternal Judgment: Part One

This lesson will be in two parts. First we will cover the revelation of God as judge. The next lesson will deal with the last judgment.

Hebrews 6:1-3 *Therefore leaving the principles of the doctrine of Christ, let us go on unto perfection; not laying again the foundation of repentance from dead works, and of faith toward God,(v. 2) Of the doctrine of baptisms, and of laying on of hands, and of resurrection of the dead, and of eternal judgment. (v. 3) And this will we do, if God permit.*

God is the righteous judge. We have been covering the six topics or applications of the doctrine of Christ. In this study we will look at the last of these foundational doctrines, "eternal judgment." God has revealed Himself in many ways. One important revelation of God is as the righteous judge.

Psalms 75:7 *But God [is] the judge: he putteth down one, and setteth up another.*

Revelation 19:11 *And I saw heaven opened, and behold a white horse; and he that sat upon him [was] called Faithful and True, and in righteousness he doth judge and make war.*

God's judgment speaks of making judicial decisions and measuring out punishment and reward accordingly.

Romans 2:16 *In the day when God shall judge the secrets of men by Jesus Christ according to my gospel.*

There will be an appointed day of judgment when God will fully judge the earth. Individuals experience temporary judgment on a personal level at different times in life, but there will be an eternal judgment at some point. Men are punished or rewarded in this life, but there will be an ultimate judgment upon men at the end of time.

Psalms 94:2 *Lift up thyself, thou judge of the earth: render a reward to the proud.*

In this verse we see that it is appropriate to pray for the judgment of God. Our prayers must in some way facilitate the righteousness of God established in the world by His judgment. God will judge the wicked and punish them for their wickedness. There is not one wicked act that shall go unpunished if that individual does not seek forgiveness in Christ. One day the scales of God's justice will be awfully and completely balanced. The wicked and the just will be thoroughly segregated. The wicked will go to eternal punishment and the righteous to reward.

Psalms 135:14 *For the LORD will judge his people, . . .*

God will judge the righteous as well as the wicked. Just because you are born of God does not mean you will not be judged. The word "judge" involves decisions. The Lord will make decisions about our lives now and our eternal disposition based on our conduct toward one another and our response to Him.

Psalms 96:10 *Say among the heathen [that] the LORD reigneth: . . . He shall judge the people righteously.*

Genesis 18:25 *. . . Shall not the Judge of all the earth do right?*

God's judgment is perfect and without flaw, and it will be thoroughly correct. He will not make one wrong decision. There will not be one error in the execution of the judgment and reward of every individual who has ever lived. Every man and woman who has ever lived will one day (individually and one at a time) give an account of himself to God.

Psalms 7:8 *The LORD shall judge the people: judge me, O LORD, according to my righteousness, and according to mine integrity [that is]* *in me.*

You do not need to fear God in His judgment. He is still the loving Father. When you know your Father, you seek His judgment rather than run from it.

Psalms 26:1 *[A Psalm] of David. Judge me, O LORD; for I have walked in mine integrity: I have trusted also in the LORD; [therefore] I shall not slide.*

Psalms 35:24 *Judge me, O LORD my God, according to thy righteousness; and let them not rejoice over me.*

Psalms 43:1 *Judge me, O God, and plead my cause against an ungodly nation: O deliver me from the deceitful and unjust man.*

Fear of judgment is an indication of an area of dishonesty in one's life or a lack of understanding of the depth of the love of God. Be honest with yourself, and continually remind yourself of the love of your Father. You need not fear Him unreasonably. You respect and live in awe of Him, but you trust and open yourself to Him with all your shortcomings, knowing that He will judge righteously and establish your heart in Him.

It is important to know that this judgment is an eternal judgment. It carries with it eternal blessing or eternal punishment. Freedom of choice will on day be taken away, and all men will be judged in the state where they are found. Those without God will be alienated from Him for eternity. Those in Christ will be caught up as fully as possible into an eternal existence and life with Him.

Chapter Twenty: Last Judgment: Part Two

In Chapter 19 we began the study of eternal judgment. The first part deals with the need for seeing the Lord not only as loving Father but also as a righteous judge. Through the Word the believer is encouraged to pray that God would judge his life and lead him on the right path. King David prayed openly for God to judge his life.

There are two kinds of judgment: (1) temporary judgment and (2) eternal judgment. Temporary judgment involves the chastening of the Lord in this life. Eternal judgment is without an end coming after death. There is reprieve in this life (on this side of eternity) when we come under the temporary judgment of God, but there is no reprieve under the eternal judgment of God after we die.

1. Temporary Judgment

Temporary judgment is not full judgment. If God were to fully judge in temporary judgment, the whole planet would be atomized in that moment. Outside of Christ the entire human race deserves nothing other than destruction. Temporary judgment is a foretaste of reward or punishment of the final judgment, which deals with the eternal disposition of the souls of men in the endless ages.

Isaiah 26:9 *With my soul have I desired thee in the night; yea, with my spirit within me will I seek thee early: for when thy judgments [are] in the earth, the inhabitants of the world will learn righteousness.*

You see here that temporary judgment is so that "the inhabitants may learn righteousness . . ." Temporary judgment is compared to a parent disciplining a child with reward and punishment to prepare him for life as an adult. Temporary judgment is God's act as Father to prepare His people for eternity with Him.

2. Final Judgment

The following passages point to God's eternal judgment.

Matthew 25:31-32 *When the Son of man shall come in his glory, and all the holy angels with him, then shall he sit upon the throne of his glory: (v. 32) And before him shall be gathered all nations: and he shall separate them one from another, as a shepherd divideth [his] sheep from the goats.*

The goat nature versus the sheep nature is described in the following verse.

Matthew 25:33 *And he shall set the sheep on his right hand, but the goats on the left.*

The right hand of God is a symbol of blessing. The left hand is a type of cursing. What is the primary difference between sheep and goats? Do you have a sheep nature or a goat nature? In using this comparison Jesus is giving us an opportunity to examine our hearts and prejudge ourselves in order to keep out of harm's way.

Sheep are followers. They need a shepherd, and they will follow him closely, submitting to his guidance and care. Goats on the other hand are isolated creatures--stubborn and unmanageable. A sheep has a settled nature, but you cannot turn your back on a goat without peril. One man said you can tell goats because they are always "butting." A goat nature is always complaining and objecting. May God give us a sheep nature and take all objection to His Word out of our lives.

Matthew 25:34 *Then shall the King say unto them on his right hand, Come, ye blessed of my Father, inherit the kingdom prepared for you from the foundation of the world.*

The Father's preparation for our success here is seen because the Father has been prepared to welcome us to our reward since before He made the earth. We were destined to walk in victory and life before Adam was ever placed in the garden. This is the Father's faith and should remove doubt and fear from our hearts as to whether we can make it in this earth walk. Your success is provided by the Father. It is up to you to take advantage of it through the promises of the Word of God.

Matthew 25:35-40 *For I was an hungred, and ye gave me meat: I was thirsty, and ye gave me drink: I was a stranger, and ye took me in: (v. 36) Naked, and ye clothed me: I was sick, and ye visited me: I was in prison, and ye came unto me. (v. 37) Then shall the righteous answer him, saying, Lord, when saw we thee an hungred, and fed [thee]? or thirsty, and gave [thee] drink? (v. 38) When saw we thee a stranger, and took [thee] in? or naked, and clothed [thee]? (v. 39) Or when saw we thee sick, or in prison, and came unto thee? (v. 40) And the King shall answer and say unto them, Verily I say unto you, Inasmuch as ye have done [it] unto one of the least of these my brethren, ye have done [it] unto me.*

Our conduct toward one another has eternal ramifications, and it is important that we be "others-oriented." In the eyes of God, how we deal with one another is a direct reflection on our love or lack of love for the Father Himself.

Matthew 25:41 *Then shall he say also unto them on the left hand, Depart from me, ye cursed, into everlasting fire, prepared for the and his angels.*

Hell is not for us. Hell is a real place. No one wants to talk about it or think of anyone going there, but these are unfortunate realities. You must also see in this verse that hell was not prepared for man. In God's plan He made provision that it might be possible that not one man would have to spend an eternity in hell. Hell was meant as the eternal prison of Satan and his minions. Because of disobedience and refusal to accept the Son of God, however, man has placed his destiny with the enemies and will join him in his destruction.

The very heart of the Gospel is giving your life away to others. The greatest discipline you can exercise is taking your thoughts and concerns to the needs of others. Even to the most lowly, your gifts, service, and love will have an eternal impact on others and upon your reward before the Father.

Matthew 25:46 *And these shall go away into everlasting punishment: but the righteous into life eternal.*

This is a time when all accounts of men are forever settled before God. Our prayer is: "Let it be our portion, Heavenly Father, to prepare ourselves now to live with You forever. Give us the wisdom to model that life for others, that we will not come empty-handed before Your throne in that day."

Chapter Twenty-one: The Fruit of the Spirit

The subject of this part of the study will be what is commonly known as the "fruits of the Spirit." We will think of them as Christian productivity in order to get away from poetic religious thinking and make the lesson very practical. The first mention of "fruits of repentance" in the New Testament is made by John the Baptist.

Matthew 3:8 *Bring forth therefore fruits meet for repentance.*

The word fruit is the Greek term *"karpos" {kar-pos'}.* It is defined as: *1) fruit; the fruit of the trees, vines, of the fields; the fruit of one's loins, i.e., his progeny, his posterity 2) that which originates or comes from something; an effect, result 2a) work, act, deed, of Christian character 2b) advantage, profit, utility 2c) praises, which are presented to God as a thank-offering 2d) to gather fruit (i.e., a reaped harvest) into life eternal (as into a granary), is used in fig. discourse of those who by their labors have fitted souls to obtain eternal life.*

By this definition it is seen that Christians are expected to be productive in their spiritual walk. The Christian life is more than agreement with religious principles or association with a religious tradition or church organization. There is in the Christian life an expectation from the Father for His children to produce actions, to deliver results, and to be profitable to His kingdom. He has planted you in the earth for the same reason a farmer plants crops--to bring forth a harvest. This can be intimidating at first glance, but you must realize what is implied by the Father when He used the term "fruits" as an analogy concerning the profit He expects us to produce in His kingdom. Fruits are produced by trees. You are one of God's trees of righteousness.

Trees do not strain to produce fruit; neither do they stand rooted on a hillside perspiring, grunting, or groaning to bring forth ripe, sweet fruit on their boughs. Very simply, they just grow fruit. It is their nature to be fruitful. They are exposed to sun, earth, and water, and as a result, they bring forth good fruit. The Scriptures call God's children trees.

Isaiah 61:3 *. . . that they might be called trees of righteousness, the planting of the LORD, that he might be glorified.*

Psalms 1:1, 3 *Blessed [is] the man that walketh not in the counsel of the ungodly, . . . (v. 3) And he shall be like a tree planted by the rivers of water, that bringeth forth his fruit in his season; his leaf also shall not wither; and whatsoever he doeth shall prosper.*

Christians produce God's expectations in their lives as He exposes them to His Word, His life, and His love. What are the fruits God is growing in His people?

Galatians 5:22-23 *But the fruit of the spirit is love, joy, peace, longsuffering, gentleness, goodness, faith, (v. 23) Meekness, temperance: against such there is no law.*

Most people capitalize the word "spirit" in this verse to indicate that these fruits are the fruits of the Holy Spirit. That is one way of looking at it, but it is probably more accurate to say that those fruits are the fruits of the born-again human spirit in union with Christ. Consider the following verse.

John 15:5 *I am the vine, ye [are] the branches: He that abideth in me, and I in him, the same bringeth forth much fruit: for without me ye can do nothing.*

Jesus is the vine or the trunk, and we are His branches. It is the branches that bear fruit, not the trunk of the vine or tree. Jesus supports us, and we produce fruit for God in response to that supporting life He imparts to us.

John 15:4 *Abide in me, and I in you. As the branch cannot bear fruit of itself, except it abide in the vine; no more can ye, except ye abide in me.*

The branch (us) cannot bear fruit unless it is in the vine (Jesus

Christ). But in Christ it is the branch (us) that bears the fruit by the life of the vine (Christ). This is a very simple analogy.

John 15:8 *Herein is my Father glorified, that ye bear much fruit; so shall ye be my disciples.*

Jesus is looking to us to bear fruit. We tend to look to Him to bear fruit in us. He is looking to us to bear fruit in Him. We should expect that we will bear fruit in Him. Apart from Him we can do nothing.

Phillipians 4:13 *I can do all things through Christ which strengtheneth me.*

Note the Father's faith toward you. You can do all things! We want to pray, "No Father, you do it. I am too weak, too humble. I cannot do anything. I am just a sinner, a mere worm . . . ." NO! A thousand times no. You are not a worm; you are a tree of righteousness. You can produce good fruit; it is your nature. Without Him you can do nothing, but you are not without Him. He lives in you and walks in you. He wants you to give Him the freedom to think through your thoughts, feel through your emotions, and take dominion of the darkness around you through your spirit that He has salvaged from sin and from Satan.

It is important to know why the Father chose to address the issue of Christian productivity using the analogy of fruit trees. He could have said, "You are my servants. I expect you to get out there and produce good works." But He did not say it like that. He says in effect, "You are my planting. You are my tree. Now, as a tree produces in an environment of sun, earth, and water, I have created you to produce just as naturally as you are exposed to the environment of My Word, My Spirit, and My Love.

This means you can relax. A tree under stress produces poorly developed, bitter fruit. Christians who are straining, working, and endeavoring to please the Father through the natural human resources of willpower and religious intimidation will never produce good fruit. Trees must be placed in the right environment to produce fruit. They need soil, air, and water. If you will simply commit to expose yourself to the spiritual elements of a Kingdom environment, you will undoubtedly produce the Father's fruit and measure up to His full expectations. What are these elements?

The Word

The Word nourishes the soul as food nourishes the body. Many times people do not read the Bible because it is boring or whatever. Even when you do not seem to get much out of Bible reading or have time for an in-depth study, you will be surprised how, in a time of need, some Scripture you scanned lightly over previously will surface in your spirit and give you just the comfort you need.

The Spirit

Exposure to the Spirit comes through prayer. Prayer is a set time of sitting quietly and opening yourself to communication with God. However, prayer is always a continual openness in the back of your mind to thoughts of His love, His character, and His nature. Prayer and the Word are essential elements for trees of righteousness, and these must be kept in balance. My grandmother, Birdie Walden, often said, "Prayer without the Word leads to emotionalism," and "The Word without prayer leads to legalism." Prayer and the Word are like the breath of the body. We breathe in the Word and breath out prayer. Both are necessary, and both must be in balance.

The Church

Fruit trees are grown most often in orchards. Believers should also be grouped together. In this manner the keepers or pastors that the Lord appoints to care for His trees can care for them and help them be fruitful. I would not want to be just a backyard apple tree. Most of those apples wind up rotten on the ground. The greatest benefit of a tree's fruit goes to others rather than itself.

Understanding Times of Fruitlessness

II Timothy 4:2 *. . . be instant in season, out of season.*

Finally, this verse points out a very helpful truth. Trees do not produce fruit 12 months out of the year. If there is a particular fruit not coming forth in your life, do not condemn yourself. You may be out of season. This does not mean that you need not demonstrate love, peace, joy, or other fruits just because you are not naturally producing that fruit at that time. Whether you feel loving at the moment or not, you should love out of obedience. That is not hypocrisy, it is obedience. At the same time, do not condemn yourself or allow yourself to be condemned for a lack in some spiritual area of your life. There is a season of fruitfulness. Be patient, and wait for it.

All the straining and striving will only diminish your potential for fruitfulness. Enter into His rest and trust the environment the Father has provided for you. He holds Himself responsible to see that you are a fruit-producing tree in His orchard. The specific fruits of the Spirit will be covered in the coming lessons.

Chapter Twenty-Two: The Fruit of Love

You are studying what is commonly known as the "fruits of the Spirit." Most people capitalize the word "spirit" in the term "fruits of the Spirit." That is one way, however, it is also said that those fruits are the fruits of the born-again human spirit in union with Christ.

John 15:5 *I am the vine, ye [are] the branches: He that abideth in me, and I in him, the same bringeth forth much fruit: for without me ye can do nothing.*

Jesus is the vine (or the trunk), and we are His branches. It is the branches that bear fruit and not the vine or the trunk of a tree.

John 15:4 *Abide in me, and I in you. As the branch cannot bear fruit of itself, except it abide in the vine; no more can ye, except ye abide in me.*

The branch (you) cannot bear fruit unless it is on the vine (Jesus Christ). But in Christ it is the branch (you) that bears the fruit by the life of the vine (Christ). This is a very simple analogy.

John 15:8 *Herein is my Father glorified, that ye bear much fruit; so shall ye be my disciples.*

Jesus is looking to you to bear fruit. You tend to look to Him to bear fruit in you, but He is looking to you to bear fruit in Him. You should expect that you will bear fruit IN HIM. Apart from Him you can do nothing.

Introduction to the Fruit of Love

Let us begin to look at the fruits of the Spirit.

Galatians 5:22-23 *But the fruit of the Spirit is love, joy, peace, longsuffering, gentleness, goodness, faith, (v. 23) Meekness, temperance: against such there is no law.*

Paul lists nine fruits or products of the Spirit. Remember that these fruits are what the influence of the Spirit of God manifests in our life and our spirit. Let us look at the love of God that the Holy Spirit causes to flow to you and through you.

The word for “love” here is *agape*, pronounced ag-ah'-pay. It means a “love feast.” Another place in Galatians says that "God is love," or agape. Agape is the "God kind of love." Theologians speak of agape as the "unconditional love of God." From these statements you can see the giving nature of the love of God. It is unprejudiced, unbiased, freely given love.

God’s Love to Us and Through Us

This is love that God causes to flow to us and through us to others. The word agape comes from the root Greek word “agapao,” which means "beloved, to be fond of, to love dearly, to be contented with.” Now, unless you receive the love of God in your own life, you will not be able to cause that love to flow out to others. You cannot give to others what you have not received for yourself. You must see now that God is agape. He has agapao for you. You are His beloved.

The Fondness of God

God is fond of you. It is not just what He does or feels toward you, but it is what He is. This is the difference--you can change what you do, but you cannot change who you are. God is love, and as you receive Him as love, you will move from love as a work (or something you do) to something that you are for you will be like your Father. He is love--you are to love. He is love in fullness--you are love in seed form. As you receive His love, this seed will grow and produce fruit in its fullness. Others will then receive that love, and the love of God will be communicated to others through you because you have received the love of God to you.

The dictionary defines "fondness" to be “loving and foolishly tender.” God is foolishly tender toward you. A further definition shows that He is "overly affectionate" toward you as a "doting" Father. As the object of God's fondness, it means that He cherishes you with strong or unreasoning affection. This means that the Father does not love you as a result of a choice He has made because He has reasoned or computed your loveableness. No, He loves you instinctively, unconditionally, and without regard for your state or situation. This is His genuine affection for you. As you receive this love, it will germinate within you and in due season begin to be produced as a spiritual fruit that others can benefit from in your life.

How the Love of God Manifests Through You

John, who wrote the Gospel of John, was known as "John the beloved." He had a deep revelation of the love of Christ toward his person from the beginning. He was known to lay his head on Jesus' shoulder during meals with the Master and His Disciples. He speaks of the love of God 39 times in his Gospel. In reviewing some of these references, you will understand the love of God toward you and how it will manifest through you to others.

John 3:16 *For God so loved the world, that he gave . . .*

God loved the world that was in total opposition to Him. He loved His enemies because love was not a choice to Him. Love is what God is, not what He does. Because God loves, He gives. He is a giving God. He does not think about giving; He gives to you intuitively and without thinking. He does not stop to decide if you deserve what you have asked. He said that, "Whatever you ask for you will receive if you only believe . . . . " As His love begins to pervade our personality and be produced in us, you will take on a giving nature. Love for you will be a natural response. Love that involves a choice, however, is not God's love. As you meditate and ponder the love of God and allow it to dominate how you think on a daily basis, you will become the personification of love even as God is love.

John 3:35 *The Father loveth the Son, and hath given all things into his hand.*

Here again is the love of God with an immediate association to giving. God is love. God is a giving God. His intuitive response to the object of His love is to give whatever is needed or desired. If you love your grandchildren or babies and give them the desires of their heart, how much more does the Father love you and is willing to give liberally to you. This is the heart of our faith for answered prayer.

John 5:20 *For the Father loveth the Son, and sheweth him all things . . .*

When you need understanding or wisdom, you need to know that you are asking the God of love. Because He loves you He will show you all the things you need to know. He says He gives because "the Father loveth." His love is the reason He gives, not your worth or holiness. For our part His love is unconditional; His love is the only condition for His giving to you as His children.

John 13:34 *A new commandment I give unto you, That ye Love one another; as I have loved you, that ye also love one another.*

You have been commanded to love others as Christ loves you. And, in reality your abundance of love or lack of love for others is an indication of your understanding of God's love for you. You see also in this verse that it is possible for you to love others with the magnitude and character of God's love. The Father would not command you to love unless He was prepared to impart to you the ability to love with His love and to bring you into a place with Him that you would grow into the personification of love even as He is love.

Continuing in the Love of God

John 15:9 *As the Father hath loved me, so have I loved you: continue ye in my love.*

It is necessary to continue in the love of God. This word "continue" means to "remain in, to survive, to hold in a particular state." You will have opportunity to depart from the love of God, but you can say in that temptation, "I will remain in the love of God." You can say within yourself, "I will not personify hostility or hatred but will remain in the personification of the love of God."

The definition of "continue" also means to "survive" in the love of God. In truth you will not survive any other way for God's faith works by love. If you allow yourself to be moved out of the love of God, you will not survive the trials of life. The way to remain in the love of God is to keep your eyes or your attention focused on what the Word says about the love of God for you even when circumstances may seem to indicate that maybe God does not love you. As you stay focused on His love, this love will begin to flow out through you to others.

Chapter Twenty-Three: The Fruit of Joy

The Fruit of Joy

Galatians 5:22 *But the fruit of the Spirit is love, joy, peace, longsuffering, gentleness, goodness, faith.*

The word for joy is the following Greek word "chara." In other places in the New Testament, this word is translated as "joy, gladness, joyful, joyous, joyfulness, joyfully." This joy is a by-product of being spiritually located in Christ as a limb or branch is located on a trunk or vine.

Joy Is Not Necessarily Happiness

Do not confuse the joy of the Lord with happiness. Happiness is a state of mind based on your happenings. Joy is a fruit of the Spirit which is present regardless of circumstances, and you must distinguish between them. You can be very unhappy but be full of the joy of the Lord. Joy is a thing produced in you because you are spiritually located with Christ. It is spiritual. Happiness is in the mental or emotional realm of your life. Emotions are fleeting, but spiritual things are lasting and consistent.

Some people have never known that the option of joy was open to them. They have been trained to base their state of mind on their emotional condition rather than their spiritual condition. God wants you to learn how to live out of your Spirit man rather than your emotions. Emotions are cruel taskmasters; they demand instant gratification and will torment a man's soul until they are satisfied. Because joy is a fruit of the Spirit, you can understand that it is your nature in Christ to produce the fruit of joy. Fruit is not produced by sweat, effort, and toil. Fruit is produced when the tree is put in an environment conducive to productivity. Let us examine the conditions necessary for you to expose yourself to the bloom, development, and ripening of the fullness of the joy of God in your life.

Promoting Joy in Your Life

I Chronicles 29:9 Then the people rejoiced, for that they offered willingly, because with perfect heart they offered willingly to the LORD: and David the king also rejoiced with great joy.

Joy is seen in this verse as something arising in the lives of those that give out of themselves toward God and the work of God. These people were spontaneous and wholehearted in their giving and worship. It was not taught as a duty but as a privilege. As you let your walk with God move from a religion to a life experience and relationship with Jesus Christ, joy will begin to be produced in your life.

Ezra 3:12 But many of the priests and Levites and chief of the fathers, [who were] ancient men, that had seen the first house, when the foundation of this house was laid before their eyes, wept with a loud voice; and many shouted aloud for joy . . .

The priests and Levites in Ezra's day rejoiced and were filled with joy because they had a deep involvement in the house of the Lord. The Lord's house in that day was a building. Today the house of the Lord is one comprised of every born-again believer in Jesus and the local churches where they assemble. It is essential to those suffering depression and loneliness not to isolate themselves. When you are hurting and dry in your spirit, the last thing you may want to do is get up and go around people or be in a crowd. But, there are great benefits accrued to your inner man from the Spirit of God by joining yourselves to fellow Christians in singing and studying together the Word of God. Isolation and separation will only promote more of the same and leave you without a support system in times of stress, i.e., when the affairs of your life bring pressures upon you that you cannot bear alone.

Esther 8:16 *The Jews had light, and gladness, and joy, and honour.*

In Esther's day the Jewish nation had light that brought joy and gladness. Light is representative of God's Word, His Spirit, and also His church.

The Word Is Light

Psalms 119:105 *Thy word [is] a lamp unto my feet, and a light unto my path.*

As you meditate on the Word of God, you will gain a perspective on the affairs of life that will register hope, faith, and confidence on your emotions. Your emotions respond to your thoughts. If you fill your thoughts with the promises of God's Word, His faithfulness, and His love, your emotions with respond accordingly.

God's Presence Is Light

I John 1:5 *This then is the message which we have heard of him, and declare unto you, that God is light, and in him is no darkness at all.*

Time spent sitting in communication and meditation in God's presence will bring joy. Remember that without light a fruit tree will not only fail to produce fruit, but it will die. Light is essential to growth of plants, and the Lord compares you with a plant when He says, "I am the vine, you are the branches."

God's People Are Light

Matthew 5:14 *Ye are the light of the world. A city that is set on an hill cannot be hid.*

The Bible speaks of the world as people that sit in darkness. If you surround yourself with people who grope through life full of self-pity, emptiness, and radical self-interest, you are causing yourself to be spiritually impaired. There is an influence of God's Spirit essential to your development that can only come by associating with positive, faith-filled, like-minded believers in Jesus.

Psalms 30:5 *. . . weeping may endure for a night, but joy [cometh] in the morning.*

Finally, be reminded that even healthy fruit trees do not

produce fruit year-round; there will be seasons of inactivity. There will be times that you will not have corresponding feelings of joy and rejoicing in your walk with Jesus. This is only a temporary condition that should be expected to pass within a reasonable time. However, if you look back on your life and find you have been consistently depressed and weighted down spiritually, then look at the environment you have surrounding yourself. Are you willing to change in order to have the full fruit of your relationship with Jesus? Or, would you rather continue in misery in order to keep up appearances?

Father, I pray for the readers that they would be filled with the joy of Lord in all circumstances. Cause them to have the faith to make any necessary adjustments in their lives to put themselves in an environment conducive to full fruitfulness in your Spirit. Heal the dryness and emptiness that they may be feeling at this time in their lives, and help them to know that fullness of joy is their portion in You as it is what you died to make available to them by your blood and the cross.

Chapter Twenty-Four: The Fruit of Peace

Galatians 5:22 *But the fruit of the Spirit is love, joy, peace, longsuffering, gentleness, goodness, faith.*

The word "peace" comes from a Greek word, "eirene." In other places in the Bible this word is translated as "rest, oneness, and quietness." As you remain in cooperation with the Father, there will be a sense of tranquility, harmony, safety, and security that will manifest itself as a residue of your intimate relationship with Jesus Christ.

Make no mistake here. This peace that God speaks of is not the absence of discord. Peace is not the absence of conflict; it is a fruit of your human spirit in communion with the Spirit of the living God. You can be in the midst of conflict, turmoil, and trouble and be perfectly composed and quiet in your inner spirit.

Philippians 4:7 *And the peace of God, which passeth all understanding, shall keep your hearts and minds through Christ Jesus.*

The fruit of peace produced in your life will transcend your circumstances. The word "understanding" here speaks of your reasoning faculty, your feelings, purposes, and desires. To say the peace of God passes understanding means that you can know peace and quietness of spirit in the midst of confusing, tumultuous events in life that would otherwise devastate you.

Men often say, "If I could understand why this is happening to me, I could deal with it." That is a wrong thought. This assumes that knowledge is power, and understanding a problem will give you the ability to solve it. The Scriptures say that you do not have the power to turn one hair of your head from white to black. This is a delivering truth. You do not have to understand the peace of God to enjoy its benefits.

God understands your problem. He knows the end from the beginning. What He wants to develop in your spirit is a trust in His perspective on your problem. He sees your need, and He will care for you. Your circumstance did not take Him by surprise, so you can trust that the God who is love is faithfully tending to your affairs. That sense of quiet, rest, and peace then rises up out of the turmoil of your life, freeing you from worry and fear.

Colossians 3:15 *And let the peace of God rule in your hearts, to the which also ye are called in one body; and be ye thankful.*

Remember that peace is a fruit of the Spirit. As a fruit, it comes forth independent of the will of man or religious striving. It is something that you "let rule in your heart . . ." rather than something you work up or conjure up through mental effort. Just relax, and let the peace of God rule you in the midst of conflict. In His earth walk Jesus went through what you are going through, and it did not affect Him the way it may be devastating you. He lives in you, therefore, He is in the midst of your conflict right along with you. He is not bouncing off the walls nor tearing His tissue into a million shreds, fretting over this particular difficulty. Let the peace that rules His heart rule your heart. It is a choice you make by training your thoughts on His viewpoint rather than your own.

II Thessalonians 1:2 *Grace unto you, and peace, from God our Father and the Lord Jesus Christ.*

Peace is something that comes from God and not from any person, circumstance, etc. It is a by-product of abiding in the vine. Because the Word of God says so, it is within you. Rather than being overwhelmed by the raging fear and torment Satan would fill you with, it is now your opportunity to let this peace begin to rule in your heart.

II Peter 1:2 *Grace and peace be multiplied unto you through the knowledge of God, and of Jesus our Lord.*

Fear came to you through knowledge of your circumstance. Peace will come to you through your knowledge of God and of His work in your behalf through Jesus Christ's death, burial, and resurrection. The multiplication of God's peace is the opposite of panic. Panic is what you experience as fear is multiplied to you. It robs you of reason, reducing you to senseless hysteria. The peace of God begins as a witness and mounts up into a pervasive, overpowering sense of composure that gives you boldness to laugh in the teeth of the tallest Goliath.

Psalms 37:11 *But the meek shall inherit the earth; and shall delight themselves in the abundance of peace.*

The meek shall delight themselves in an abundance of peace. The word "meek" means humble. Do you know what humility is? The Lord spoke to me years ago that humility is not condemning yourself and saying derogatory things about yourself. Humility is agreeing with what God says about you and your circumstance. Humility says: "I am who God says I am. I am redeemed. I am saved. I am safe from sickness, poverty, and strife. I am what He says I am. I am His child. I am that which He died to deliver from the domain of darkness into the kingdom of the Son of God's love."

If you will agree with God and what he says about you and your circumstance, you will begin to experience a residue of peace and a fullness of quiet rest in your spirit. This is your heritage, and it is the promise of God for you. Accept it now as yours, and claim it as your provision in the midst of whatever circumstance you may find yourself.

Psalms 55:18 *He hath delivered my soul in peace from the battle [that was] against me: for there were many with me.*

Chapter Twenty-Five: The Fruit of Patience

Galatians 5:22 *But the fruit of the Spirit is love, joy, peace, longsuffering, gentleness, goodness, faith.*

Let us begin to study the longsuffering that is produced in the born-again man via the in-born nature of God within man. The Greek definition for "longsuffering" is *patience, endurance, constancy, steadfastness, perseverance; slowness in avenging wrongs*. It is said, "Don't pray for patience because you will get tribulation." Jesus had this to say about tribulation in the following Scripture.

John 16:33 *These things I have spoken unto you, that in me ye might have peace. In the world ye shall have tribulation: but be of good cheer; I have overcome the world.*

You will have tribulation whether you pray for patience or not. Patience is the key to receiving from God. If your patience runs out and you give up, then all of your previous faith and sacrifice are of no avail.

Hebrews 10:36 *For ye have need of patience, that, after ye have done the will of God, ye might receive the promise.*

Patience is the only thing that will keep you after you have fulfilled the will of God. When you have done all you can do in a situation and you have obeyed to the best of your knowledge and the answer has yet to arrive, the fruit of patience will sustain you till the answer comes. Do not give up just before the answer comes. Patience is the quality that will sustain you and keep you from making that error.

Luke 8:15 *But that on the good ground are they, which in an honest and good heart, having heard the word, keep [it], and bring forth fruit with patience.*

According to this verse it is not faith that brings the manifestation of the promise. Faith plants the seed, but it is patience which brings forth the harvest. Faith conceives the substance; patience brings forth the manifestation. Patience is the fruit of the Spirit that works along with you, sustaining your expectation of God's blessing being made manifest in your life.

James 5:7 *Be patient therefore, brethren, unto the coming of the Lord. Behold, the husbandman waiteth for the precious fruit of the earth, and hath long patience for it, until he receive the early and latter rain.*

The coming of the Lord in this verse is not just speaking of His coming at the end of time. It applies to Him showing up in the form of answered prayer in the midst of your circumstance.

The Bible continually speaks of patience in agricultural terms. The farmer has long patience for the harvest because he knows the quality of the seed that he planted. The strength of your patience is measured by your confidence in the seed. The seed is the Word of God.

Luke 8:11 *Now the parable is this: The seed is the word of God.*

I Peter 1:23 *Being born again, not of corruptible seed, but of incorruptible, by the word of God, which liveth and abideth for ever.*

The Word of God is an incorruptible seed. No matter where you plant it, the Word will bring forth if you will be patient. When you pray, invoke the Word of God. Say what God says about your circumstance. Pray the answers found in God's Word. Do not pray the problem. If you pray the problem, that is what you have planted, and that which you have planted will bring forth in abundance. What you pray is what you plant.

Praying the problem will relieve the stress but, at the same time, open the door to the devil because you planted the problem rather than planting the Word. Go find a promise in God's Word that applies to your situation and then thank the Father that He made provision for your circumstance. Claim the promise for your own, and expect a harvest of blessing for your prayers.

Next, wait patiently. Patience works out in your life as you claim endurance without complaint. As you are waiting on the answer, the situation will come to mind often. You will be tempted to complain or begin to have fear. When this happens, open your mouth, and thank the Lord for the answer. Thank Him for the goodness of His Word. Then, go about your business. Do not always be figuring out how God is going to answer; just know that He will answer. Do not go digging up the seeds of prayer and then wonder why they all died and never produced answers. Leave them in the ground of your heart, and let the seeds produce in God's time.

Mark 4:26-27 *And he said, So is the kingdom of God, as if a man should cast seed into the ground; (v. 27) And should sleep, and rise night and day, and the seed should spring and grow up, he knoweth not how.*

When you are waiting for the manifestation of answered prayer, just go about your business and know that the seed and the ground will work. Have enough faith to go to bed and get up.

Mark 4:28 *For the earth bringeth forth fruit of herself; first the blade, then the ear, after that the full corn in the ear.*

The earth [the heart of man] will bring forth by itself. But, there is a process involved. The blade brings the promise of fruit. The blade represents the inward assurance of answered prayer. The ear points to circumstances that begin to line up in your live concerning what you are praying about. You begin to see the direction that God is going to answer your need; finally, the full manifestation of the answer you act on and see is fully met.

Patience is the key. Patience is leaving the seed alone, not picking too early and not settling for second best. Let the full, mature answer to prayer come forth, and when it is fully available, take the action that is involved in taking advantage of the provisions God has made for you.

Father, I thank you that patience brings forth the answer to the prayers prayed in faith. Give us the patience that is long in waiting and never acts too soon or gives up the fight. We receive the full harvest of answered prayer, and thank you for the wisdom to wait on your Word to bring about the harvest of blessing your Son died to provide us. Amen.

Chapter Twenty-six: The Fruit of Gentleness

Galatians 5:22 *But the fruit of the Spirit is love, joy, peace, longsuffering, gentleness, goodness, faith.*

We discussed in an earlier lesson that the capitalization of the word "spirit" here was put in by the translators but was not in the original language of this letter. Jesus said that He was the vine, and we are the branches. He spoke of us abiding in Him in order to bear much fruit. Our connection to Jesus is a spiritual connection, and the fruit of that communion is spiritual fruit or, as we see here, the fruit of the human spirit in union with God's Holy Spirit. The love, joy, peace, etc., are fruits or qualities that are produced in our lives as a result of union with Him.

The manner in which this fruit blossoms, matures, and comes to fullness is exactly parallel to what is involved in a natural fruit tree producing fruit. In fact, the Bible often speaks of the believer as a tree of righteousness of the Lord's planting and so on.

The Fruit of Gentleness

The Greek word for gentleness in the New Testament is as follows: *1) fit, fit for use, useful; virtuous, good; 2) manageable, i.e. mild, pleasant (as opp. to harsh, hard; sharp, bitter) of things: more pleasant toward people, kind, benevolent.*

Now, look at this quality as a product of your intimacy with Christ. As you abide in Him, there is a kindness (an easiness) that will begin to evidence itself in your personality. You will become more manageable, mild, pleasant, and generally more fit company for your fellow human beings! When you see Him as He is, then you will be like Him. Your personality is a reflection of the spirit to which you are most exposed. The spirit of religious Christianity is a severe, small-minded, temperamental spirit that has nothing to do with God, who is love.

You cannot give away to others the gentleness you have never allowed the Father to show you. You cannot exhibit to the world what you have never allowed the Father to demonstrate to you. King David spoke vividly of the kindness and gentleness of the Father in the following verse.

II ***Samuel 22:36*** *Thou hast also given me the shield of thy salvation: and thy gentleness hath made me great.*

The Hebrew word "gentle" means to "stoop low." In effect David is saying, "Father, you lowered your expectations and brought me into a relationship with you. And, the result is that I have become great." Again, what David saw in God he personified as a result of his relationship with the Father. The Father always makes the first move. He does not demand you to measure up to His standards before He is intimate with you; quite the opposite is true. He sees intimacy with mankind as the means by which He will cause His creation to become what He is.

How does this work? Because you know the Father lowered Himself to make you great, you are willing to lower your expectations toward others. Because He made the first move toward you, you are willing to make the first move toward people you would otherwise resent because of their attitude toward you. There is so much heartbreak and loneliness in the body of Christ because of a deficit of understanding in this one area.

If you are waiting for the other brother or sister to make the first move toward you, you are expecting something from them that you can only receive from the Father. That is idolatry.

Romans 5:8 *But God commendeth his love toward us, in that, while we were yet sinners, Christ died for us.*

***Ephesians 4:1-2** I, therefore, the prisoner of the Lord, beseech you that ye walk worthy of the vocation wherewith ye are called, (v. 2) With all lowliness and meekness, with longsuffering, forbearing one another in love.*

The word love here is “agape” which means "fondness, over-affection, to be foolishly tender." You cannot give this love away unless you have first received it yourself. This is the love that Paul said in Galatians that is “God is.” Yet, you probably have a view of the Father that is somewhat different from the lover that this word implies. It is time to let God love you and to let His tenderness influence you. In man's eyes the Father's love is foolishly tender, therefore, they have contrived an old, white-haired man (rather than a doting Father) on a distant throne. The result is a failed Christianity and a world darkened in sin and hate.

There is hope, however, in the harvest of love and gentleness developed and born out in the life of one like you, abiding in Christ and bearing this fruit in your season. Let it happen. Let him love you, and let him love others through you. The result will be a fulfilled life and will achieve the purpose of God in planting you in so deep a love and affection that it could only be expressed by the gift of Christ’s life on the cross.

Chapter Twenty-Seven: The Fruit of Goodness

Galatians 5:22 *But the fruit of the Spirit is love, joy, peace, longsuffering, gentleness, goodness, faith.*

This study approaches the subject of goodness as a fruit of the Spirit. What is spiritual goodness? Sometimes when you see what something is not, you see more clearly what it is. It is not something attained by human will. Because it is spoken of as a fruit, you must realize that the human will is not involved. Only plants bear fruit.

In the analogies of the Scripture speaking of spirituality in terms of trees and plants, you must note that these subjects address spiritual issues that do not involve the human will. Will is involved, but not the "human will." God has planted you in His vineyard and determined that you will bear fruit. He has rooted you in His love, bathed you in the warmth of His presence, and watered you with His Word. That which is produced in you (as the fruits of the spirit) speaks of the will and patience of the Father, rather than human will and faithfulness originating in yourself.

Faith, itself, is a fruit of the Spirit. That means the urge to will to do good and the drive to carry that will out to completion are themselves processes initiated not in your will but in the will and mind of God. The Scriptures say that no man seeks after God.

John 6:44 *No man can come to me, except the Father which hath sent me draw him.*

Christianity today has been out of touch with the heart of the Father and the essence of His power. Therefore, Christianity has wrongfully lifted up the power of man's will as the agent utilized to cause man to fulfill the Father's will.

Let us define the word "goodness" from this verse in Galatians.

The Greek word is where we derive the woman's name "Agatha." *Goodness (4); 1) uprightness of heart and life, goodness, kindness*. This term comes from a similar word: *agathos {ag-ath-os'} 1) of good constitution or nature 2) useful, salutary 3) good, pleasant, agreeable, joyful, happy 4) excellent, distinguished; 5) upright, honorable.*

You can draw from these definitions that the fruit of goodness in the life of a Christian involves a certain air of pleasantness, of being easy to get along with. Rather curious, then, is that Christianity is better known for its squabbles and holy wars than for its unity and harmony.

This word also carries the import of a life lived in "usefulness" and is experienced as "salutary." In everyday Christianity, however, its most visible activity is no activity at all but passively sitting by being sermonized once a week. This is not said in spite but to reinforce what the Scriptures describe as life in Christ. What modern religion espouses as life in Christ are two entirely different things. From a Biblical perspective we are living far below our privileges.

Another word for goodness in this verse is similar to the one above: *1) uprightness of heart and life, goodness, kindness.* Here you see a repetition of the thought of uprightness of heart. The term uprightness is very curious indeed. Today, men of letters tell us that man came from four-footed creatures and that man, by comparison, has evolved into a highly advanced state of uprightness. On the other hand, the Scriptures indicate that man was born in the image of God and has denigrated from uprightness to a low state of humiliation.

In using this word "agatha" to define a distinct fruit of the Spirit in communion with Christ, there is a strong indication of a need for a deeper understanding of uprightness in Christ. The uprightness lost in the fall was required under the law and restored under grace. As a born-again man or woman, you have deep in the core of your being the uprightness of nature that gives definition to the personality of God. The name “God” is a form of the word "good." So, goodness then becomes a matter of what you are, not so much what you do. The goodness that is a fruit of the Spirit comes out of your nature in Christ and not by striving in Christianity.

This goodness speaks of excellence and dignity of bearing. This is again a fruit of communion with Christ. The heart and life are wrapped up in a personal relationship with Christ, and the by-product of that intimacy is this thing called goodness. Christianity today is so preoccupied with achieving goodness through human means that intimacy with Christ is a side issue and, in many instances, is no longer a central aspect of Christian expectation.

How does a relationship and intimacy with Christ foster the goodness of nature that causes "godliness" in a believer's character? Consider this: If you were to be placed in the company of rough-cut individuals, foul of mouth, and vile of thought for one week, you would be profoundly affected and drawn into that nature. Likewise, to place you in the company of men of learning and refinement, you would likewise be affected by their nature. Even so, to bask in the presence and personal friendship of the Father, you will ultimately begin to take on His nature, His thoughts, feelings, and purposes. This is affected through the Word, worship, and involvement with His family. Through a personal, intimate acquaintanceship, His nature becomes imbedded in your being, and there comes a point where it is difficult to distinguish where you leave off and the Father takes up. Even as He prayed in John 17, you are one.

Learn to relax, and if you serve, do it out of love for the One you are intimate. Let Him love you, and in that love relationship there will come an equalization of your character with His, and your personality will become shaped by His kindness, dignity, and goodness.

Chapter Twenty-Eight: The Fruit of Faith

What is Faith? Faith is spoken of as a fruit of the Spirit in Galatians 5:22. It is also spoken of as a gift of the Spirit In I Corinthians 12:9. The gifts of the Spirit are occasional anointings that manifest in the believer's life as God uses him/her to bless others and be a witness for the Gospel. The fruit of faith is a personal development into trust and confidence in God that results in a victorious life.

I John 5:4 *. . . and this is the victory that overcometh the world, even our faith.*

If you have faith, you have the victory. Victory is realized by the developing and releasing of your faith. Faith can come as a special anointing or gift of the Spirit. This faith is a supernatural assurance that the thing asked for is done. But this same faith is developed in you as an ongoing, indwelling assurance and confidence in the Word of God and its potential impact on your daily life. We will look at what faith is and what it is not. Sometimes when you see what something is not, what it is becomes clearer.

<u>Faith Is the Means By Which God Causes Your Hopes and Dreams to Be Realized</u>

Mark 11:24 speaks of asking the Father for what you desire. Most people only ask for what they think the Father wants for them. They pray a religious prayer that is not based on the true desires in their lives.

Hebrews 11:1 *Now faith is the substance of things hoped for, the evidence of things not seen.*

Faith can only give substance to your hopes. If you pray a dishonest prayer, you have wasted your breath. It is time to get honest with the Father concerning your wants and desires. If they are wrong, He will adjust you accordingly.

One translation reads, "Faith gives substance to things hoped for." The word "substance" means "that which has actual existence." Faith is the means by which the things you expect are given actual reality. Faith in the heart takes the place of the thing desired in your life. If you have faith, you have the answer because faith causes the answer to be made manifest in your life.

Everything God Does in the Earth Is Through Faith

As the following Scriptures show, everything God does in the earth is through faith. God made a faith world. Hebrews 11:3 tells us that God made the world through faith. It is held together by faith and continues to exist by faith, the faith of God. You are created in the image of God and, therefore, are designed to function by faith in the faith world that God created. All the New Testament miracles were accomplished by faith.

Acts 3:16 *And his name through faith in his name hath made this man strong, whom ye see and know: yea, the faith which is by him hath given him this perfect soundness in the presence of you all.*

The name of Jesus does not work by itself, otherwise, it would be a mere chant. The name of Jesus works through faith. Many churches fight over the name of Jesus; but, without faith the name of Jesus is not effective. The name of Jesus and the power in that name is released through faith--not feeling, emotion, mental philosophy, or spiritual experience.

Romans 3:25 *. . . God set [Jesus] forth [to be] a propitiation through faith in his blood, to declare his righteousness for the remission of sins that are past, through the forbearance of God.*

The mediation of Christ on the cross only becomes effective in your life through faith in His blood. His righteousness is only imparted to you on the occasion of the release of your faith.

Romans 3:30 *Seeing [it is] one God, which shall justify the circumcision* *by faith, and uncircumcision through faith.*

God has justified man (declared him just as if he had never sinned) as conditioned upon a man's faith. Everything God does is through faith. Without faith you face life as though the atheist were correct and there was no God. For outside of faith there is no reality of God in life. All God's dealings in life are through faith and based on faith.

Galatians 3:14 *That the blessing of Abraham might come on the Gentiles through Jesus Christ; that we might receive the promise of the Spirit through faith.*

All the promises of God are activated in your life through faith. This faith is a special gift that can be activated spontaneously, but it is also a quality developed in your inward man through intimacy with God and acquaintance with His Word. The gift of faith will come and go, but the fruit of faith, when developed, is always available and a sure resource in time of need.

Ephesians 2:8 *For by grace are ye saved through faith; and that not of yourselves: [it is] the gift of God.*

The grace of God saves, secures, delivers, and provides for you through faith. Without faith there could be no grace. Grace is unavailable outside of faith but is something that God has obligated Himself to develop in your life--it is His gift.

II Timothy 3:15 *And that from a child thou hast known the holy scriptures, which are able to make thee wise unto salvation through faith which is in Christ Jesus.*

The key to understanding the Scriptures is to understand that they are designed to develop faith in the heart of the reader. The Word makes you wise concerning the salvation Christ died to make available to you through faith.

Hebrews 6:12 *That ye be not slothful, but followers of them who* *through faith and patience inherit the promises.*

Lazy people do not move in faith. We are to be followers of those whose faith is proven. You do not have time to follow a loser. Therefore, find someone moving in faith, and follow their example. In time you will get activated and become an example others will follow.

God Made the World to Operate By Faith

Hebrews 11:3 *Through faith we understand that the worlds were framed by the word of God, so that things which are seen were not made of things which do appear.*

God made a faith world. When He created the animals, they were designed to exist by following instincts. Man was designed to function in life by faith--not feeling, emotion, mental philosophy, or spiritual experience. So, when feelings or thoughts contradict your faith and the Word of God, go with the Word. Dedicate your will to the Word, and only to act on the Word. This is how you partake of the fruit of faith in your life.

Man was made in the image of God and given dominion over all the earth. As with God's image, the only example man had of taking dominion was the way God worked—through faith by His Word.

Faith Toward God Is the Base Line of the Christian Experience

Hebrews 11:33 *Who through faith subdued kingdoms, wrought righteousness, obtained promises, stopped the mouths of lions.*

Faith is the lowest common denominator of your walk with God. You must see that you have it, know how to develop it, stay in it, and know how to use it effectively in the affairs of your life.

Faith Is the Primary Requirement for a Relationship With God

Hebrews 11:6 *But without faith [it is] impossible to please [him]: for he that cometh to God must believe that he is, and [that] he is a rewarder*

of them that diligently seek him.

Faith Is Allowing God to Represent Himself to Us in the Word

Faith is not just believing who God is in human terms, but faith is who God is as He has represented himself to us in the Word. God is Love. He is our Provider. He is our Healer. He is our victory in the circumstances of life. He is our Comforter. He is our Teacher. He is El-Shaddai, the All Sufficient One. He is our Peace. He is our Light. God is all things that are good and perfect as expressed in Christ Jesus, who died on the cross and rose again in order to provide a means by which He can live in us and through us. He has given us mastery in Himself over circumstances, over principalities and powers, over sickness, disease, and poverty. God transforms us in our spirit and personality to perfectly express His character, nature, and power.

This is God. To believe anything else is to put yourself in a position where it is impossible to please Him no matter how emotional, warm, and tender your feelings may be toward Him. He has limited himself not to be moved by your emotions or your tears but by your faith. He did not say emotions, crying, and tear-stained prayers are the substance of things hoped for; He said faith is the substance of things hoped for.

How Faith Comes

Romans 10:17 *So then faith [cometh] by hearing, and hearing by the word of God.*

Galatians 3:2 *This only would I learn of you, Received ye the Spirit by the works of the law, or by the hearing of faith?*

In other words, good works are not the basis of God's Spirit indwelling you but rather by hearing, comprehending, and embracing the good news of Jesus Christ concerning your situation. As faith develops in you, your capacity for the indwelling of the Holy Spirit is increased as well.

Galatians 3:5 *He therefore that ministereth to you the Spirit, and worketh miracles among you, [doeth he it] by the works of the law, or by the hearing of faith?*

Even moving in the miraculous does not develop in a person's life through good works, sacrifice, or special holiness--but by faith. Anyone can develop in the faith that produces the miraculous (since miracles occur through faith). You have mountain-moving faith developing on the inside of you.

Acts 3:12 *And when Peter saw [it], he answered unto the people, Ye men of Israel, why marvel ye at this? or why look ye so earnestly on us, as though by our own power or holiness we had made this man to walk?*

Acts 3:16 *And his name through faith in his name hath made this man strong, whom ye see and know: yea, the faith which is by him hath given him this perfect soundness in the presence of you all.*

Faith--not special power--causes miracles to take place. And, you have the faith of God developing on the inside of you. Through the faith of God in His Word, the name of Jesus will come together in your life and create miracles that will transform your life and the lives of others. Your part is to cooperate and give your roots to the love of God, the water of His Word, and the sun of His presence. The result will be permanence to your faith that will bring consistency and constancy to your Christian experience.

Chapter Twenty-nine: The Fruit of Temperance

Galatians 5:23 *. . . Meekness, temperance: against such there is no law*

.

The last fruit of the spirit mentioned is temperance. Temperance is defined in the Greek lexicon as "self-control (the virtue of one who masters his desires and passions, especially his sensual appetites)." This word also carries a meaning derived from metallurgy. It refers to the hardness and elasticity imparted to steel through an intense heating and cooling process. A thing that is tempered is made less intense or violent by means of an outside influence.

Christian temperance is derived from the Spirit's influence, not will power. As a fruit of the Spirit is in union with Jesus Christ, temperance is the effect of the otherly influence of God's Spirit upon your emotions and sensibilities. In music, for example, temper deals with being tuned in accordance with some other temperament. As a fruit of the Spirit, this involves your human temperament being brought into accord and harmony with the divine temperament of God.

<u>The Problem With Will Power</u>

The self-control produced out of your relationship with Christ cannot be confused with temperance that has its root in will power. Will power, exerted against the passions of your lower nature, will bring about an outward appearance of conformity to societal expectations. But, exercising will power is like exercising the bicep--it grows stronger and more powerful. In the will this eventually results in stubbornness and an unteachable nature. Using will power to control the temper is like applying chemotherapy to a cancer patient. Both are lethal, and if the chemical treatment is even slightly maladjusted, it can take the patient's life. As a fruit of the Spirit, self-control can be described as a residual effect of exercising a personal relationship with Jesus by the indwelling of the Holy Spirit.

Christian Experiences Contrast Religious Discipline

When Paul was in prison, he spoke to Felix, a Roman official, concerning temperance.

Acts 24:25 *And as he reasoned of righteousness, temperance, and judgment to come, Felix trembled, and answered, Go thy way for this time; when I have a convenient season, I will call for thee.*

Felix, no doubt being schooled in the Greek philosophies, was greatly intimidated by Paul's message of temperance. Because of the vein in which Paul spoke in the verse above, he could ascertain Paul's message as something only truly attainable as a by-product of an intimate relationship with Jesus Christ. Christian temperance is brought into your life by focus upon him and away from yourself.

The underlying point is that the emphasis of your Christianity should be your intimacy with the Father and not the disciplines of the will. Religion finds its expression in various regimens, disciplines, and liturgies. Yet, there is an aspect of Christianity that has nothing to do with those principles but rather is a relationship no less personal or intimate than a man might have with any other man. This intimacy, so lacking in the modern faith, is the strength of all spiritual reality to be experienced in Christ. Christian disciplines, regimens, and liturgies are of no higher value than the practices of the Moslem or Hindu when they are exercised outside the context of a personal, intimate relationship with Christ.

Therefore, in your desire to address the unruly aspects of your lower nature, let your focus be upon His sufficiency and not your inadequacy. Tear your eyes away from the glaring, black malignancies of anger, lust, or hatred in your life. Instead, look to the indwelling Spirit, and meditate on the Word and the promises of God. In so doing you admit to the defeat of your human ability to become like God or to harness your sinful nature. You are saying, "If the cross was not enough, there is no point struggling against this wickedness in my nature." This is true because you have not resisted temptation in this area to the point of bloodshed (nor are you likely to in the future). But Christ gave His life on the cross as an act of delivering you from these condemning sins of lust, strife, pride, etc. As you turn to Him and commune with Him in prayer, mediation, and the Word, you will find His influence reaching across all your weaknesses, giving you supernatural leverage against the manifestations of intemperance in your life.

Chapter Thirty: The Fruit of Meekness

The next fruit of the spirit is meekness. Meekness is be produced in your life when you place yourself in an environment conducive to spiritual growth. These fruits will not be produced in your life by your willpower. They are produced as the result of the environment you place yourself in. Trees don't have a will, nor do they choose to produce fruit. Therefore by this analogy, these things of the spirit are not produced by our willpower, but by a methodology similar to the manner in which tree produce fruit.

Galatians 5:23 *Meekness, temperance: against such there is no law.*

The word for meekness means "gentleness or mildness". It is included along with the word gentleness because while gentleness deals with your attitude toward men, meekness deals with your attitude toward God. One example of meekness in the old testament is Moses. He had the following testimony:

Numbers 12:3 *(Now the man Moses [was] very meek, above all the men which [were] upon the face of the earth.)*

Now looking at the life of Moses will tell you that this ς 144 ς

____________________ ____________________

____________________ ____________________

"Meekness" had nothing to do with letting people run you over and wipe their feet on you. Moses got up in Pharaoh's face and demanded him to let his nation go. God, through this man brought this world power to its knees before him. The fruit of meekness is produced in your life as an attitude of gentle submission toward God, not a character flaw that allows any Tom, Dick or Harry run you over any time they want to.

The quality of meekness in your character will activate the blessings of God in your natural life.

Psalms 22:26 *The meek shall eat and be satisfied: they shall praise the LORD that seek him: your heart shall live for ever.*

A meek person knows when enough is enough. His posture before the Lord does not leave him ever seeking for some new experience or thrill. His sense of ambition and goals are not born of a desire to feed the ego but a commitment to glorifying the Lord. He does not seek to be praised of men, but rather that men should praise the Lord.

Psalms 25:9 *The meek will he guide in judgment: and the meek will he teach his way.*

Meekness before the Lord involves teachableness. You can't teach an arrogant man. I've counseled people whose lives are in shambles, families ripped apart, health ruined, but they will not receive counsel. They remain committed to their own way, even though it leads them to destruction. Like Elvis Presley their anthem is "I did it my way ..." Yes, he did do it his way and if you pursue your own way, you will wind up like he did.

Psalms 37:11 *But the meek shall inherit the earth; and shall delight themselves in the abundance of peace.*

S 145 S

Meekness embodies a love of peace. You may be like some folks, who don't feel alive unless they are embroiled in some mighty turmoil. If there is nothing amiss in their lives, they will 'compass sea and land' to create a crisis, for that is what they thrive on. As for the meek, they don't get bored with a peaceable existence. They delight in the order and structure of a peaceable life. They have little need to "get away from it all ..." Because they love the paths that the Father has cause them to tread on.

Psalms 45:4 *And in thy majesty ride prosperously because of truth and meekness [and] righteousness; and thy right hand shall teach thee terrible things.*

Meekness brings prosperity. A commitment to truth and a refusal to live in self deception cause a person to look hard at their lives. They take a pragmatic approach to their affairs of their existence and will not commit to something that does not work. If the family is a mess, they will go to the word and take its correction no matter how cutting. If their spiritual life is a mess, they will make any change dictated by the word no matter what family, friends think or how many enemies it will make. As a result they will find the good path of life that leads to prosperity, health and peace of mind.

Psalms 76:9 *When God arose to judgment, to save all the meek of the earth. Selah.*

There is no fear of judgement in the meek. They have 'judged themselves that they be not judged.' Therefore they do not wring their hands at the social calamity and impending doom that may hang over the world. In the midst of chaos and upheaval they rejoice and are glad, for the Word foretold these

S 146 S

things just prior to the advent of Christ. So let it come. Let the wars and rumors of war rage, let all hell break loose for your anchor is in Christ and he will be your stay, if he has to rain manna from heaven and bring water from the rock.

Zephaniah 2:3 *Seek ye the LORD, all ye meek of the earth, which have wrought his judgment; seek righteousness, seek meekness: it may be ye shall be hid in the day of the LORD'S anger.*

The meek person will be a doer of the word. They are committed to God's justice in their lives because they 'seek righteousness' or a right standing with God.

Matthew 11:29 *Take my yoke upon you, and learn of me; for I am meek and lowly in heart: and ye shall find rest unto your souls.*

Jesus is the preeminent example of meekness. Yet we see him giving scathing rebuke to the religious powers of his day. He committed assault with intent to commit bodily harm in the temple. Meekness does not mean the absence of anger. He called his own disciples a bunch of faithless perverts because of their unwillingness to have faith.

Yet he was meekness. What is the manifestation of meekness in his life.

Jesus was not stuck on himself. He simply believed who the Father said He was. Meekness believes, "I am who the Word says I am..." Many who put themselves down think they are being meek. Quite the opposite they are arrogantly denying what the word says about them. The word says you are the righteousness of God in Christ. To believe other than this, negatively or positively is an act of pride.

Jesus never advertised his ministry. He refused to allow men to exalt him. He rebuked a woman for blessing Mary, his mother.

S 147 S

He was lowly, he left the exaltation of his mission and message in the hand of the Father. Humility is an attitude toward God, not man. Peter taught that you should humble yourself to God, yet you don't see one command in scripture to humble yourself to man. However if you are humble toward God you will have a gentleness toward your fellow man.

Meekness is your posture before God. Biblical meekness has no comparison to what the world calls meekness. It has nothing to do with letting the world run you over. Moses and Jesus, the highest examples of meekness were bold and unswerving in their rebuke and resistance against ungodliness and religion. Yet their lives were only reflection of the Father's will, not their own willfulness. Meekness does not sap the vitality of a strong personality. Rather it is harnessed for the Father's use. Allow that harness to slip over you in order that you may inherit the land the Father has promised you.

Chapter Thirty-one: The Need for God's Gifts

A great embarrassment among Christians is a predicament one man described as "the eternal childhood of the believer." For years I prayed and asked God to give me "milk" for the spiritual babes in my flock. I did not understand at that time why I had so many immature Christians in my care, and yet their complaints and cries implied that many of their needs were going unmet. Then a travelling minister made an observation that began to shed light on my questions.

Many people that remain in immaturity are actually just neglected sheep! There is something in the "spiritual genetics" of the spiritually retarded that causes them to be incapable of maturing beyond the rank of infancy. They have been trained by the institutions and churches that fostered them to sit flaccidly in the pew like cattle in a livestock yard. They exist merely to further the attendance goals of the organizations they are in and to make their leader, priest, or pastor look good. They have no sense of destiny and no personal mission from Christ beyond their regular feedings and burpings on Sunday morning.

When will the Christian grow up? Simply put, they will grow up when God's pattern for personal relatedness to His Son and His purpose in the earth are taken by every Christian individual as a matter of personal accountability.

Romans 12:1-2 *I beseech you therefore, brethren, by the mercies of God, that ye present your bodies a living sacrifice, holy, acceptable unto God, which is your reasonable service. (v. 2) And be not conformed to this world: but be ye transformed by the renewing of your mind, that ye may prove what is that good, and acceptable, and perfect, will of God.*

According to Romans 12:1-2, it is reasonable in God's eye that you should give yourself (body and soul) as a sacrifice in His service. Yet, the altar of surrender is not to be one of your own choosing but rather a place of service ordained in the fabric of His plan from before the foundations of the world. It is this "giving" of yourself that is the bench mark of your maturity. And, this giving out of your life is meant to be facilitated by your relationship to the local church.

What is the church? In the eyes of God, the church in any community is seen as the relationship that exists between all born-again believers. It is the sum total of all believers in that locality that God acknowledges as His candlestick. It is not a building, an organization, or a non-profit corporation. It may involve all of these, but ultimately "the church" is held by God to be a community within the community that is expected to be rightly related to Him, to one another, and to the unsaved in that area.

Ephisians 4:1 *Therefore, the prisoner of the Lord, beseech you that ye walk worthy of the vocation wherewith ye are called.*

Your place in this relationship is spoken of in Ephesians 4:1 as your "vocation" in Christ. This is a vocation exercised as you: *(v. 24) "consider one another to provoke unto love and to good works: (v. 25) not forsaking the assembling of yourselves together . . ."* (Hebrews 10:24-25). God expects you to participate in giving attentive, continuous care to watching over your fellow Christians and bearing witness of Christ to the unredeemed in your community. The verification of your maturity in Christ is the acceptance of this portion of the ministry.

At some point every believer must be initiated into service to Christ in the area where God has called him. Your ministry portion as a Christian will involve three areas of God's gifts:

1. Ministry gifts
2. Charismatic gifts
3. Motivational gifts

The leadership of the local church is intended by the Father to be the influence in your life that shapes, molds, and provokes you to fulfill your personal calling. By anointing these people to serve as examples before His church, God breaks into the human relationships of the church and gives opportunity for men to follow Him by following those He has delegated before them as pastors and leaders.

Your pastors and elders are the most spiritual people in the local church (at least they should be if they have been ordained of God and not man). God has put a calling upon their lives that drives them to passionately preach the Gospel and stand before the people in His name. Paul said, *". . . woe is unto me, if I preach not the gospel!"* (I Corinthians 9:16).

To rightly relate to these gifts Christ has given you, you must involve yourself with them. Hebrews 10:25 tells us to assemble together for the purpose of being ministered to and to minister. "Assembling together" is more than just coming together under one roof. The word implies coming together as members of the body of Christ. Each one has his place or his membership. The failure of the modern church to "assemble" has turned the church into a passive crowd rather than a dynamic spiritual family. The church is seen as somewhere we go to endure, for a span of time, the intonation of a liturgy or sermon. Then, off you go in pursuit of your own life until religious tradition demands your attendance once again.

The five-fold ministry of Ephesians 4:11-16 is:

1. Apostle
2. Prophet
3. Evangelist
4. Pastor
5. Teacher

God uses these offices and gifts to initiate the urging, warning, encouraging process by which He matures the saints. Ignorant men have claimed that most of these gifts have passed, but they have no Scriptural ground for this deception. As long as there is need to mature in Christ, there is need for these ministries.

It is through these vessels that God intervenes upon the human relationships of the Christian community and imparts a passion for Him and a love for others in the body. Through the five-fold ministry, God molds and mouths the concepts of the message of His love and the manifestation of His power. There is no possibility of growing up into Christ without the influence of these men in your life. To deny these gifts is to deny the God that gave them.

I Samuel 8:7 *And the Lord said unto Samuel . . . they have not rejected thee, but they have rejected me, that I should not reign over them.*

These ministries are foundational to the individual Christian and the Christian family. They provide stability for growth. They are not a "covering" as is wrongly taught by many, but they are undergirding those who Christ personally covers. The church is not built around or under the apostles and prophets but according to Ephesians 2:21-22 are built on them. Jesus does not need a pope or chief apostle that only magnifies himself at the expense of the people.

The measure of maturity according to Ephesians 4:13 is that we might develop until we all attain oneness in the faith and in the comprehension of the full and accurate knowledge of the Son of God and that we might arrive at really mature manhood--completeness of personality--which is nothing less than the standard height of Christ's own perfection, the measure of the stature of the fullness of the Christ, and the completeness found in Him. This is not a state you will achieve when you die and go to heaven. This state is brought about by God through the ministry of the apostles, prophets, evangelists, pastors, and teachers.

Chapter Thirty-two: The Gift of the Apostles

The word “apostle” has no English equivalent. To readers of the New Testament, the term itself has an aura of mystery that we must look through to understand that Jesus calls ordinary men today as He did then to function as apostles.

The definition of the word apostle is: "a delegate; one who is sent with full power of attorney to act in the place of another, the sender remaining behind to back up the one sent." An apostle is sent by God to do what He Himself would do in a place, a situation, or among a people.

Most of the church world today thinks in terms of the twelve men Jesus left His Gospel as the only true apostles. Yet, Jesus currently calls men by the Holy Spirit to do the same job as the first apostles. Apostles are a gift given to the church in every generation. A popular argument against modern day apostles is that their function was to write Scripture, and since we have the Bible, there is no need for apostles. Let it be noted, however, that Nathanael, Philip, and Andrew were apostles as was Timothy and Titus, yet none of these wrote one word of Scripture. Instead, all were called and ordained along with the other apostles and sent out to lay foundations for churches to grow.

Jesus gave these men to the Christian community-at-large. Jesus is the giver of the Holy Spirit, and, in turn, the Holy Spirit gives Christ's gifts to the whole congregation. Jesus gives us the gifts of these men who He calls and ordains to function in the local assembly. These men are principally men endowed with a deep, personal revelation of Jesus Christ such as Paul and Peter received from the Father.

Ephesians 4:12-13 *For the perfecting of the saints, for the work of the ministry, for the edifying of the body of Christ: (v. 13) Till we all come in the unity of the faith, a perfect man, unto the measure of the stature of the fullness of Christ.*

These men have a clear-cut ministry to the church. Even as the Holy Spirit comes with His gifts, so do these men come with gifts. Please notice that today's church needs the same ministry as the Ephesian church. How can we know this? Simply because Ephesians 4:13 has not yet been fulfilled.

If you are born again and desire to grow up into Christ, the influence of an apostle will be necessary. Paul goes on to say in Ephesians 4:14, *"That we henceforth be no more children, tossed to and fro, and carried about with every wind of doctrine . . . .* " An apostle will also make demands on you to grow up and to stop being childish in the things of God.

<u>The Apostolic Commission</u>

Mark 3:14-15 And he ordained twelve, that they should be with him, and that he might send them forth to preach, (v. 15) And to have power to heal sicknesses, and to cast out devils.

The apostolic commission is first stated by Jesus in Mark 3:14. Jesus called the Apostles to Himself to be with Him; that He might send them forth to preach and to have power to heal sickness and to cast out devils. Simply stated, the apostle preaches the Word of God with signs following. He further ordains elders or overseers to care for the flock. He then could go and repeat the process of planting churches once more. After His resurrection Jesus gave the eleven this commission once again.

In I Corinthians Paul states that God first set the apostles in the church as "master builders and foundation layers." Ephesians 2:20 indicates that while Jesus is the cornerstone of the church, He extends this foundational ministry through the apostles and prophets. This applies to the Old Testament prophets, the New Testament apostles, and modern apostles and prophets.

<u>The Man Jesus Chooses</u>

The original twelve "apostles of the lamb" were plain, ordinary men. Likewise, the "apostles of the spirit" are simple and common in their background. Paul (a homicidal fanatic in the vein of Hitler or Manson) was the first apostle of the spirit when Christ called and transformed him to God's service. Remember, the apostle is not the head of the church; Paul was a part of the foundation and that is why God set them first in the church. You do not build a house until the foundation is laid and, then, construction toward the roof may begin.

The Churches Responsibility Toward the Apostles

Revelation 2:17 *He that hast an ear, let him hear what the Spirit saith unto the churches; To him that overcometh I will give to eat of the hidden manna, and will give him a white stone, and in the stone a new name written, which no man knoweth saving he that receiveth it.*

The church at Ephesus was the assembly to whom Paul articulated the teaching of the five-fold ministry. In Revelation 2:17 this same church is commended by Jesus for exposing false apostles. This remarkable church not only survived the infiltration of false apostles, but it exposed them and destroyed their influence. We must accept the same task today. God is raising up true apostles. However, Satan counterfeits every move of God by bringing forth his anti-apostles. The false apostles must be exposed and cut off from their access to the flock.

A few thoughts about current apostolic ministry will help. The early apostles were founding apostles in a fledgling church. The last-day apostles have been identified rightly as being "finishing apostles." They minister in a different setting and culture, but the fatherly ministry of the current apostles is the same. Current apostles are concerned with establishing new churches locally and strengthening established churches. An apostle is not simply a missionary. At home and abroad, apostles are needed anywhere there are saints in need of maturing or fields ripe for church planting. Today's apostles can be seen as emerging apostles. Few, however, are operating in the power of the spirit and magnitude of the early apostles, but this is to be expected.

There are apostolic traits in certain ministries. One striking aspect is a care for the pastors in their area of ministry. The apostle is very much the "pastor's pastor." This is a great blessing but can also bring confusion if the pastor is easily threatened or the apostle get overbearing. They must be allowed to make mistakes. They should be corrected, not rejected. God's anointing rests on who they are and what they do to develop themselves for strengthening the church.

Chapter Thirty-three: The Gift of the Prophets

In II Chronicles 20:20, King Jehoshaphat stood before his people and declared:

> *. . . Hear me, O Judah, and ye inhabitants of Jerusalem; Believe in the Lord your God, so shall ye be established; believe his prophets, so shall ye prosper.*

An overview of the church today reveals a great many people who are less than prosperous. Christianity hovers on the periphery of society more and more with little real influence or power. The fact that the world often influences the Christian to a greater degree than the church influences the world is a painful reality. The bars and dance halls are full, yet the church pews are often vacant. In England less than 10% of the population remotely acknowledge Christian beliefs in any form. In America 64% of the population acknowledge a Christian belief, however, only an infinitesimal part of this percentage is even marginally active in any church life.

In spite of the public relations hype of the religious institutions of our day, the church and Christianity are a pitiful caricature of the glorious church Christ promised upon His return. The modern church has a great need to be exposed to valid prophetic influence, and it is just this influence that the Father is making more and more available in our day.

<u>If the Foundations Be Destroyed</u>

Psalms 11:3 *If the foundations be destroyed, what can the righteous do?*

Ephesians 2:19-20 *Now therefore ye . . . (v.20) . . . are built upon the foundation of the apostles and prophets, Jesus Christ himself being the chief corner stone.*

The religious crowd of the day has rejected the foundation upon which God would construct His church. Even in full gospel circles, a minister is only acknowledged as a pastor or evangelist. If he declares a prophetic or apostolic calling, he is wrongly regarded as "puffed up, presumptuous, or in error."

This rejection of the prophetic ministry is typical of the religious system of our day. The book of Revelation symbolizes the established religious systems of our time to be Babylon. In Revelation 18 the destruction of these systems are foretold.

Revelation 18:20 *Rejoice over her, thou heaven, and ye holy apostles and prophets; for God hath avenged you on her.*

This Scripture gives us a key to discovering the Babylon church today. She is a system that opposes the ministry of the prophet and apostle. Notice that the verse does not tell the pastors, evangelists, or teacher to rejoice. Babylon does not persecute those ministries--she rails and mocks the ministry of the prophets and the apostles. Why? because Satan knows the Word. If he cannot get the churches to reject Jesus, he will tempt them to reject those ministers in whom Jesus invests and shares His foundation ministry. Babylon is not simply the Catholic Church as protestants are fond of saying, but it is any church system that rejects any God-given ministry.

The Road to Restoration

Those concerned about moving the church back to a Biblical model for Christianity must be prepared to acknowledge the ministries of prophets and apostles. These must be identified and validated, and the false ministries must be exposed without rejecting the genuine ministries.

First Apostles, Secondarily Prophets

I Corinthians 12:28 *And God hath set some in the church, first apostles, secondarily prophets.*

This verse does not apply to Old Testament prophets because they predated the Apostles. It, therefore, confirms the existence of the New Testament prophetic ministry. While the apostle ministry is spoken of by Paul as an office, the prophetic ministry is described as an anointing and also a set ministry. Why is this important to understand? Because Paul was only an apostle to the group he was called to by God (i.e., the Gentiles). A prophet, however, is a prophet wherever he travels because prophetic ministry emphasizes anointing rather than office.

The apostolic ministry was spoken of by Paul as having "a measure" or limit to its jurisdiction. Therefore, if a great apostle in Michigan visited a church in Louisiana, he would only be a traveling brother. A prophet, on the other hand, is a prophet wherever he goes for his prophetic ministry flows out of an abiding anointing in his life.

The Prophet's Job

The prophet's role involves him in the morale of the people of God. The apostle commissions the people to a vision; the prophet motivates the people to commit to the mission; the evangelist recruits new people to the vision; the teacher instructs us on how to carry the mission out; and, the pastor cares for our emotional and other needs during the carrying out of the mission. A prophet, therefore, reinforces right motivations and actions and speaks against wrong motivations and actions among those he is sent to by God.

Nathan and David

II Samuel 7:2-3 *That the king said unto Nathan the prophet, See now, I dwell in an house of cedar, but the ark of God dwelleth within curtains. (v. 3) And Nathan said to the king, Go, do all that is in thine heart; for the Lord is with thee.*

In II Samuel 7:2-3, we find King David is motivated to build the Lord a house or temple, and Nathan's response as a prophet is that of encouragement. As a Christian when you are striving to serve the Lord, the prophet's in your assembly will reinforce the good intentions of your heart. The prophets will lift you up and instruct you through their counsel and through words of wisdom and knowledge.

In II Samuel 12:1-7, however, King David has committed murder and adultery. The prophet Nathan exposes David's hidden sin and speaks against David's wrong motives and actions. If you have sin in your life that is not dealt with, the Lord may, in fact, use a prophet to bring you to repentance. At times the words of a prophet may seem challenging and too personal, but he will always speak from an abiding love for his brothers. The heart of a prophet grieves over sin and luke-warmness in the fellowship and rejoices when God's people respond to Christ in dedication and service.

Prophets are men that motivate and inspire people. They minister from the context of their own personalities. Sometimes they are quiet and still; other times raging and torrential like John the Baptist. The prophet proclaims a message, speaking openly to men on behalf of God. Along with the apostles, they are foundational to the church. They are "forth-tellers" of what the Lord has said more than "fore-tellers" of what the future holds although that is part of their ministry as well. They prophesy to groups as well as individuals, and they will submit their prophecies to the judgment of the local church to which they are connected.

Chapter Thirty-four: Evangelist, Pastor, Teacher

The ministry gifts are given by God in Ephesians 4:11-14. His purpose was that Christ “be formed" in men as recorded in Galatians 4:19.

Galatians 4:19 *My little children, of whom I travail in birth again until Christ be formed in you.*

Through these gifts Christians can attain to a maturity described as the "full measure of Christ." The gifts are for the "perfecting of the saints." These men are not given to do the work of the ministry but rather that they would mature the saints in order that they themselves would do the work they have come to expect of the ministry.

The ministries must be present in the church. The believer will not mature properly if he is not exposed to each of the five ministries of Christ. These ministries are foundational to the structure of the church and essential to the health of the believer. The church without these gifts is crippled in her attempts to obey the great commission.

The Evangelist

Let us define the gift of the evangelist. The word "evangelist” is derived from the Greek word "evangelistes" and means “a messenger of good." It describes a man or woman who is known as a "preacher of good tidings."

The word “preach” is defined “Evangelizo.” Another word for preach is "to publish" (see Matthew 3:1; Mark 1:45; Luke 4:18-19). This could conceivably describe a writer or an author. Webster's dictionary defines the word preach as "to speak publicly for another--an intercessor . . . ."

The term "advocate" is a contemporary word for the Biblical

word "intercessor." He is one who pleads or speaks for another. So, we can conclude that a key function of the evangelist is to be a prayer warrior, an intercessor. (see Isaiah 52:7)

Another word for preach is "Parrhesiazomai." This word is found in Acts 9:27 and means to be "very bold in speech." The evangelist, then, would tend to be very demonstrative, direct, and forceful in his message. Remember that the evangelist as a five-fold ministry is primarily for the maturing of the saints. Consequently, we must understand that his preaching work is not done "for us" but rather as an example "to us" on how we should carry on the work of evangelism ourselves.

The Pastor

The word in the Bible for "pastor" is "poimen." This is a shepherd, one who feeds and tends herds or flocks. He is not merely one who feeds, but he also tends to the needs of the flock.

The role we define as pastoral today is really a combination of pastor, prophet, and apostle. The modern pastor usually works alone and is expected to be all of these roles plus many others as well. The early church, on the other hand, was set up with teams of leaders called "elders." There was never mention of one man being the pastor or priest. The modern applications of these offices are extra-Biblical and does not promote adherence to the Biblical pattern for church life.

Ideally, the entire five ministries should be in every local assembly. A pastor should not be expected to be a "one-man band." Jesus also sent workers out two-by-two. There is no instance of New Testament workers traveling or laboring alone. This condition has precipitated many the scandals and failures in the churches today.

The Bishop

The word "bishop" implies one who "protects, looks over, inspects, or take oversight." Jesus is spoken of as the "bishop of our souls." The bishop ministry is equivalent to the ministry of the apostle.

The Elder

The word for “elder” is very close to the same meaning as "bishop." The difference in the early church was that a bishop was usually a man who traveled to an area to establish a church; whereas, an elder was a man who (with other elders) was appointed to care for the church in his home area.

Was Peter the first Pope? In I Peter 5, Peter says that he is a "fellow elder" and a "co-laborer." This was his function. He saw himself as a peer of the other elders and bishops in the first-century church. He submitted to them and even received rebuke from them when he fell into error in the book of Acts. There is no indication in early church history that Peter exercised autocratic leadership over the affairs of primitive Christianity.

Hierarchical Systems

The system of leadership in the church today is hierarchical. Here, the pastor bottlenecks the leadership of the church and exercises nonscriptural authority over the lives of others. Jesus said in Revelation that He hated the deeds of the Nicolaitans. This was a sect, who divided the church into clergy and laity. The word “clergy” mean "sacred," whereas the word "laity" means "common" or "profane." After the deaths of the apostles, this doctrine of demons infiltrated the church and still shapes the leadership structure of Christian religions today.

The Teacher

The gift of teaching is also for the maturing of the saints. The teacher's gift is to explain the Word of God precisely and accurately. A teacher wants to bring the saints to a deeper understanding of the Word of God. He is more informational than inspirational. This may lead to a “dry” presentation. However, the teacher is a defense against false doctrine creeping into the teachings of the church.

Chapter Thirty-five: The Gifts of Revelation

This lesson introduces what is generally known as the "charismatic gifts" or the "nine gifts of the Spirit." There are certainly more than nine, but these are grouped together nicely. When seen in operation, they are very dramatic in their impact on the needs of people to whom they are addressed. For the sake of this study, these gifts are considered in groups of three. The categories are: (1) the spoken or utterance gifts; (2) the power gifts; and (3) the gifts of revelation. This lesson will cover the revelation gifts.

Every believer has a call and gifting from God. These nine gifts will operate in the lives of most believers who seek to cultivate them for God's service. As you study, open your heart to the activation of these ministry gifts in your life for the good of those in need.

The Gifts of Revelation

<u>The Eyes of God</u>

The gifts of revelation are the word of wisdom, the word of knowledge, and discernment of spirits. These gifts are endowments of supernatural insight into otherwise inscrutable situations. These gifts cause one to see a person or a situation as God sees the person or situation.

Although primarily a seeing gift, speech is required in order to communicate these discernments. These gifts meet the Christians' need for having God's insight into their circumstances. They are not perceptions for the rational mind. A person cannot think them up or communicate them on his own. They operate from a perception beyond the rationale or natural mind. Information that comes from the revelation gifts comes from outside the bounds of the natural thinking processes--information which your mind does not conceive, or your ears do not hear, or your eyes do not see.

If the church was moving in the spiritual gifts of revelation, there would be no need for fortune tellers, crystal ball gazers, etc. These counterfeits have become widespread because the church has neglected or rejected altogether God's legitimate gifts of insight and revelation.

The Word of Wisdom

A word of wisdom is an utterance inspired by God and spoken by an individual. It reveals a part of the total wisdom of God. It is "seeing" what God sees in a situation and saying it. It is applying God's wisdom to a specific situation.

In I Kings 3:16-28, you observe the word of wisdom in operation in Solomon's life. Two harlots were brought to Solomon with one child. Both claimed the child to be their own. The word of wisdom came to Solomon, and he ordered the child to be cut in half. The result was that the true mother was revealed by her compassion. The observation of the people was that the spirit of wisdom was in Solomon to execute judgment in Israel. The word of wisdom will never glorify men--it will always glorify God.

Another instance in which you will observe the word of wisdom is found in I Corinthians 5:1-5. Paul judged the matter at hand by the word of wisdom even though he had no information in the natural. He judged "by the Spirit." A man was involved in an incestuous relationship in the church, and the leaders refused to deal with it. The word of wisdom came that the solution was to turn the offender over to Satan. The result was that the Corinthian church obeyed and the offender was ultimately reconciled. (II Corinthians 2:6-9).

In Matthew 22:15-22, the Pharisees tried to trick Jesus in His teachings in order to arrest Him. They asked Him whether it was right to pay tribute to Caesar. The word of wisdom came when Jesus asked whose image was on the coin, that they should give Caesar what was his own, and give God what was due Him. The result again was that the people marveled at God's wisdom in Jesus.

The church at Jerusalem in Acts 15:5-27 was up in arms over the issue of circumcision for non-Jews. There was great contention and debate. James, operating in the word of wisdom, said, "Do not trouble the Gentiles . . . but write to abstain . . . ." The result was that God brought agreement and unity where there was strife and anger.

The word of wisdom will come when you are in any kind of situation which requires problem solving. This gift will also operate in a counseling setting. What some preachers call "revelation knowledge" that comes spontaneously when they are at the pulpit is really a word of wisdom in operation.

How does a word of wisdom come? It will come when you perceive God's viewpoint on what is about to be done or said in a given situation. It will come as a picture in your mind's eye. Sometimes this comes following a word of knowledge concerning something accompanied by a confirmation of the Lord's will in that situation by a word of wisdom. A word of wisdom is a "how to" piece of information given by the Holy Spirit concerning a specific situation in your life or the life of someone to whom you are ministering.

Personal Prophecy and the Word of Wisdom

There is much controversy today over "personal prophecy." This gift is administered concerning personal affairs to an individual. It is usually very directive in its subject matter and is accompanied by a word of knowledge about the person's past and a foretelling of this individual's near future. While these words are prophetic in nature, they are not prophecy by a strict interpretation. II Peter 1:20 states that no prophecy is of "private interpretation." These prophecies are very personal and highly subjective as to their application and interpretation. These "words" then are words of wisdom or God's perspective on the issues addressed in this person's life.

The Word of Knowledge

The word of knowledge is an utterance inspired by God and

spoken by an individual. It is an insight into the events and circumstances surrounding a situation at hand. This insight proceeds from the Spirit of God and will not involve information gathered from natural means. This gift shares the truth of facts which the Spirit wishes declared concerning a specific occasion with a practical application of confirming God's love and awareness to all concerned.

In Colossians 2:1-5, Paul gives a powerful example of the word of knowledge in operation. The Colossian church was one among many that Paul had not visited personally. Paul was concerned that these churches were properly set in order. Therefore, by the Spirit through the word of knowledge, Paul "beheld their order" and, therefore, approved of them sight unseen. Paul wrote the whole book of Colossians on the basis of the operation of the word of knowledge. Then, in Colossians 4:2 Paul tells how he did it when he said, *"Continue in prayer, and watch in the same . . . ."* The word of knowledge functions strongly in the prayer life of the believer.

The Satanic counterfeit of the word of knowledge is astral projection or soul travel. The exception is that the believer does not leave his body when the word of knowledge operates. The Holy Spirit is all knowing and omnipresent. He lives in the believer, and from time to time through the word of knowledge, He communicates supernaturally acquired intelligence to you concerning affairs in your life or the lives of others.

Two classic examples of the word of knowledge are found in John 4:7-25 and II Samuel 12:1-7. The first example is where Jesus told the woman at the well all about herself and the second is where Nathan the prophet went to David and exposed his sin concerning Bathsheba.

A word of knowledge may come in public or private settings. A word of knowledge may be expected whenever God's insight is needed. Words of knowledge may reveal sin, help locate lost items (car keys, etc.), warn or provide safety (take the bus rather than drive yourself to work), reveal thoughts, provide healing, or provide instruction.

How does a word of knowledge come? A word of knowledge will come to you as pictures in your mind's eye or as an intuition. This is an inner knowing, perhaps a picture of a written word. In the case of a word of knowledge for healing, it may come in the form of a pain in the body. It may also come as a spontaneous utterance which flows out almost without your volition. So, you see it, know it, read it, feel it, or say it.

The Discerning of Spirits

Discerning of spirits is the supernatural capacity to judge from a spiritual insight whether the spirit operation in a given situation is human, divine, or demonic. It is a supernatural perception into spiritual activity.

1. Discerning Human Spirits. In I Samuel 16:6-13, God helped Samuel discern which of Jesse's sons was to be king. The gift of discernment of spirits operated as an inner voice instructing Samuel how to choose the Lord's anointed.

   In John 1:43 Jesus discerned the guileless nature of Nathaniel. The result was that faith was stirred up in Nathaniel to believe that Jesus was the Christ.

2. Discerning God's Spirit. Eli, the High Priest, discerned in I Samuel 3:1-9 that the voice calling to the child, Samuel, was the voice of the Lord. Peter discerned by the Spirit that Jesus was the Christ in Matthew 16:17-20.
3. Discerning Demonic Spirits. In Matthew 16:21-23, Jesus discerned that Satan was speaking through Peter, seeking to discourage Him from going to the cross. For three days Paul allowed a woman to praise them publicly until he discerned that she was inspired by a demon spirit (Acts 16:16-18).

Expect discerning of spirits when a prophecy, tongues, interpretation, or other gifts are in operation; when a conflict or disturbance arises in a ministry setting; when there is possible demonic activity; or perhaps in a public or private setting.

How Does Discernment of Spirits Come?

Discernment of a human spirit may come as a word written over the face. It may also come as an irresistible knowledge of the spirit of the person involved (i.e., seeing through them as though they were transparent).

Discernment of the Spirit of God may come by seeing the anointing on an individual. This is often a glowing or a light flitting across one's face. It can also be as a cloud over the face or seeing an angelic figure standing nearby. The Holy Spirit may also be discerned as a sweet smell in the air around a person.

Discernment of a demonic spirit may come by a foul smell. Often, demonic activity is discerned as dark shadows or a patch of darkness on a face. Discernment may also come as a sudden, strong temptation (such as anger or lust). Care must be taken to distinguish between personal weakness and demonic activity. Discernment here may also come in an open vision of demonic activity.

To act on the gift of discernment, first of all “pray.” Go to the leaders responsible in the church or in an individual's home. Keep your mouth shut. Many times God will reveal flaws and vulnerabilities in those around you to test your integrity and commitment to those individuals. Many who claim to have discernment are only acting on their own suspicions. Judge yourself clearly first. This gift (above all others) can be abused and bring chaos into a situation. Some people will "discern" a prophecy or other gift as not of God, yet these same people have never operated in the gifts themselves.

How can you discern if someone else's gift is not of God when you cannot obey the Spirit when He prompts you to prophesy? You cannot, of course. In these instances the "discernment" is actually an exposure of fears and spiritual bigotry in your own life. You should be bold to operate in this useful gift but also use discretion so as not to harm others. There is wisdom in a multitude of counselors. When in doubt, get the opinion of a designated leader and/or a close friend and then act appropriately.

Chapter Thirty-six: The Gifts of Power: Signs, Miracles, and Wonders

Jesus prophesied of a people whose testimony would be confirmed by signs, miracles, and wonders.

Mark 16:17-18 *And these signs shall follow them that believe; In my name shall they cast out devils; they shall speak with new tongues; (v. 18) They shall take up serpents; and if they drink any deadly thing, it shall not hurt them; they shall lay hands on the sick, and they shall recover.*

If you are not one of these that Jesus speaks of, you are living far below your privileges as a child of God. In John 14:12 Jesus spoke of a company of believers who would not only do the things that He did but would go on in the power of the Spirit to do even greater things. The writers of the New Testament tasted of this "greater things" ministry. The writing of the Bible itself was a greater work because Jesus never wrote anything for posterity. Therefore, in His church (His living temple), Jesus continues a ministry that does greater things than He did on the earth. The early church only tasted of this ministry. The book of Joel shows us what this "greater things" ministry will look like in full bloom at the end of the church age before Jesus returns.

Joel 2:28-31 *And it shall come to pass afterward, that I will pour out my spirit upon all flesh; and your sons and your daughters shall prophesy, your old men shall dream dreams, your young men shall see vision: (v. 29) And also upon the servants and upon the handmaids in those days will I pour out my spirit. (v. 30) And I will shew wonders in the heavens and in the earth, blood, and fire, and pillars of smoke. (v. 31) The sun shall be turned into darkness, and the moon into blood, before the great and terrible day of the Lord come.*

The Best Is Yet to Come

Peter spoke of the Pentecostal outpouring as being that which

Joel prophesied about in Acts 2:16. Yet, church history tells us that this prophecy was not completely fulfilled in the early church. They tasted but did not experience the fullness of the outpouring of the Holy Spirit. Nor has any generation since seen a total fulfillment of Joel's prophecy. Notice that the Holy Spirit through Joel states that this ministry will come to pass before that great and notable day of the Lord--before the church is taken out of the earth.

You, therefore, can see that you and I have a great, promised outpouring of the Spirit which is coming upon the church and the world. At the command of God, the sun will turn to darkness. At the meetings of God's people will be seen pillars of smoke and of fire. The Spirit will be poured out in prophecy, visions, wonders, and signs in the heavens and the earth. These signs will not just happen automatically; rather, they will be effected by the believers who will go forth into all the world preaching the Gospel. And these marvelous signs will follow them in an end-time revival that will bring a harvest of souls as has never been witnessed throughout church history.

The Power Gifts

With the above introduction you can come with anticipation and excitement to this study of the power gifts of the Spirit. These gifts have been available for generations, but because of neglect, unbelief, and luke-warmness, they have been very little in evidence. Remember that if you have been born of the Spirit, you have access to the gifts because these gifts are all in the Holy Spirit. They are His, and He has made them available to those who earnestly desire spiritual gifts.

Faith, Healing, and Miracles

The gifts of faith, healings, and miracles are the gifts in which the power of God is seen. They are acts of God through which His divine energy accomplishes a particular result in word or work. So you see that the revelation gifts *unveil* something, the utterance gifts *say* something, and the power gifts *do* something.

All Gifts Work in Clusters

It would be good at this point to recognize that the nine gifts of the Spirit manifest in groups or clusters. Rarely will one gift stand alone. Here is one scenario I have often experienced:

> I received a word of knowledge that a certain woman in the audience was in need of a gift of healing. I called her to the front and minstered to her, and she "fell under the power" (the gift of miracles).

This is most common in the operation of the gifts--they complement one another. When one individual is ministering, there are often scores of others in the audience who are receiving tongues, prophecies, words of knowledge, etc. So do not ever hesitate to minster even when someone else has already ministered.

I Corinthians 14:*30 If any thing be revealed to another that sitteth by, let the first hold his peace.*

The Gift of Faith

This gift is the bestowal of supernatural confidence in the face of seeming impossible obstacles. The receptor is enabled by the Spirit to believe for what he otherwise could not believe. To experience this gift is to lose consciousness of "having faith" or "exercising faith." The needed answer becomes as real as the ground under your feet or the air you breathe.

Read Acts 3:1-7. Peter operated in the gift of faith when he raised up the man at the gate Beautiful. He said, ". . . such as I have . . . I give you." He did not tell the man what Jesus usually did (i.e., ". . . according to your faith, so be it to you . . . "). This man was going to receive regardless of whether he personally believed or not. Peter had the gift of faith for both of them. Notice that this gift worked in conjunction with the gift of miracles.

Personal Experience. A few years ago my wife and I went through a time of great financial stress. At one point there were no groceries and no money. The children were crying from hunger. We did not know what we were going to do. I sensed the gift of faith in manifestation. I told her to go down the hall to the kitchen and boil some water for a chicken stew. We did not have any chicken. We did not have a crumb in the cupboard. No one knew our need. We made a practice of only letting God know what we needed. Before the water boiled, we had two chickens and $244 dollars for groceries. A lady who had visited the church once was compelled to get up and come to the parsonage with those two chickens and that money. This was the gift of faith in operation.

Another time my wife and I prayed for a person with diabetes. There was no outward change, but I was totally assured of this man's healing. He never took another dose of insulin.

I was a candidate at a certain church in need of a minister. The members approached me to pray whether or not I was their next pastor. I knew the Lord would cause them to vote for me 100 percent. That night it happened just like I believed. Some members later reported they intended to vote against me but were supernaturally restrained and voted in favor of my candidacy as their pastor.

The gift of faith is a surge of confidence that arises within a person faced with a specified need or situation. It gives that person a certainty and assurance of the answer to a prayer or need. It is the irresistible knowledge of God's intervention at a certain point and the accompanying authority to act through the power of the Spirit in miracles, healing, or another gift.

The Gift of Miracles

This gift involves the suspension of natural laws by the spirit of God to bring testimony to His name. A miracle is an event in which people and things are visibly and beneficially affected in an extraordinary way by the power of God.

The Greek word for miracle is "dunamis" or "power." This suggests that the operation of this gift comes as the Spirit gives a person the capacity to carry out some event in a spontaneous expression of power. The difference between the gift of faith and the gift of miracles is this--faith receives, but miracles work or perform. When my wife and I needed groceries, the gift of faith operated, and we received through a supernatural manifestation of faith.

What follows is one example of the gift of miracles versus faith. I was with a group of young Christians on an outing when a very dark and threatening storm approached. The group broke up and ran for their cars. Inspired by the challenge, I stood before this storm front and commanded the clouds to lift in the name of Jesus. I commanded the rain to cease. In spite of the storm warning and the black sky, it did not rain. In fact, it did not rain for three weeks. Only when the Lord directed me to pray for rain did the dry spell break. In fact, it began to pour down rain within fifteen minutes of my prayer.

One common manifestation of miracles is what we call being slain in the Spirit. This is a sign gift whereby a person swoons (faints) under the amplified anointing of God on his physical body. I have seen scores of people fall and hit their head hard enough to inflict a mild concussion. Never once have I even seen a bruise on these individuals. God intervenes upon them in a manifestation of supernatural power.

When Jesus turned the water into wine in John 2:1-11, the gift of miracles was in operation. When He cursed the fig tree in Mark 11:12-22, the gift of miracles was also in operation.

The Gifts of Healing

These gifts are the actual healing events a sick person receives. These gifts can come spontaneously or progressively. As there are many kinds of sicknesses, so there are many gifts of healings. Healing is the event or progression by which a sick person receives restoration of the body or mind.

Mark 16:18 *. . . they shall lay hands on the sick, and they shall recover.*

Note in this passage that healing comes by the laying on of hands. James 5:14 prescribes prayer and the anointing with oil. Jesus spit in some peoples' eyes and put mud in the eyes of others. He spoke only a word at other times, and many times He laid His hands on the sick to heal them. There is no one formula that is required. Healing is a work of the Spirit.

The above passage also speaks of the result of laying on of hands as "they shall recover." This implies a passage of time. I have been fairly successful when laying hands on people with tumors, cancer, diabetes, barrenness, and infectious diseases. With other ailments we have not seen as many healings. As you pray for the sick, you will discover in due time what gifts of healing manifest in your life. Each one of us will have great results in one area and perhaps poorer success in others. This reveals that we all need one another. No one person can minster alone. The gifts of the Spirit function in the context of the Christian family and the local church. We learn to submit in love to the ministry of Christ in each other.

Healing in Operation. The gift of healing comes as we reach out in love to the sick and needy. I ministered to one girl in an isolation room at the hospital. She had hepatitis and mononucleosis. The devil tried to put fear in us of catching these very diseases if we put our hands on her. We went in anyway and laid hands on her. She was dismissed the next day totally healed.

Another man was terminally ill. The day before we came the doctor had given him three months to live. There was no cure for his illness. We went in and prayed for him, and he was miraculously healed. He walked out of the hospital a few days later. The gift of healing requires obedience. You must step out and give God the opportunity to use you in this gift.

Another case I saw was a young lady with a brain tumor. We called her out in a meeting and told her by the Spirit exactly what her need was and what the doctor had said. Then, we prayed in faith for the gift of healing to operate. She returned for more tests with the doctors, and they found nothing.

Time and again I have seen healing come. One common denominator was that we made ourselves available by stepping out in faith to minister to the sick. We also prayed for the gifts of healing to operate through us. We coveted the gifts of healing according to Scripture, and they have continued to operate.

<u>Sensitivity Is Important</u>. The power gifts demand great boldness at times. There are often questions in the mind, a veritable storm of "what if." You do not have to have all the answers--just be willing to obey and leave the results to the Lord. Move in sensitivity, and yield to the Spirit. Above all, take up the challenge of faith. Your job is to obey, and God's job is to back up your obedience with signs following.

Chapter Thirty-seven: The Utterance Gifts Prophecy

What is prophecy? Prophecy is a tool God uses to stir His people. It is the most important of the utterance gifts. The reason for this is that it takes the other two (tongues and interpretation) to equal this one gift. When you mature in the utterance gifts, you will generally not give a message in tongues unless the Lord wants someone else to interpret or use as a sign to the unbeliever.

I Corinthians 14:22 *Wherefore tongues are for a sign, not to them that believe, but to them that believe not: but prophesying serveth not for them that believe not, but for them which believe.*

Prophecy is a supernatural utterance in a known tongue. The Hebrew word for "prophesy" means to "flow forth." It also carries the thought, "to bubble like a fountain, to let drop, to lift up, to tumble forth, to spring forth." The Greek word means "to speak for God" a "verbal communication of the mind of God, originating from divine inspiration."

<u>Who Should Prophesy</u>?

I Corinthains 14:1 *Follow after charity, and desire spiritual gifts, but rather that ye may prophesy."*

Everyone in the church from the youngest to the oldest should prophesy. Prophecy is a pre-eminent gift because:

I Corinthians 14:3 *But he that prophesieth speaketh unto men to edification, and exhortation, and comfort.*

The early church gives us a pattern for modern church life. Prophesy and the open ministry of every Christian was the rule. The teaching of one man to a silent audience was a great exception.

I Corinthians 14:26 *How is it then, brethren? when ye come together, every one of you hath a psalm, hath a doctrine, hath a tongue, hath a revelation, hath an interpretation. Let all things be done unto edifying.*

The usual contention here is that the meeting must be conducted decently and in order. The idea of everyone ministering in the gathering drowns the religious mind into offense and unbelief. This objection is a perversion of the following verse.

I Corinthians 14:40 *Let all things be done decently and in order.*

Without a doubt Paul is demanding decent, orderly conduct in the gathering. In this passage, however, he is actually calling for two things to be done. First, let "all things" be done (psalms, doctrines, revelations) from the assembled group; and, secondly, let these things be done in decency and in order.

If a modern church does not fulfill both aspects of this command, it is holding an indecent and disorderly meeting even if they have three songs, take the offering, preach 20 minutes, and go home! According to Paul the religious spirit promotes this kind of thinking and perverts God's intentions for gathering.

What Is Prophecy For?

I Corinthians 14:3 *But he that prophesieth speaketh unto men to edification, and exhortation, and comfort.*

In other words, prophecy is to be used as a tool of encouragement. You should always leave the church edified and lifted up in hope and motivation to face spiritual challenges. Many times this may not happen at the time a prophecy is given. The reason for this is that the word may deal with negatives that leave the group heavy-hearted. But, the result of acting on the word (in repentance, forgiveness, etc.) will bring about edification and comfort.

What Prophecy Is Not

Prophecy is not for doctrine, or soapbox grandstanding, or telling everyone off with a "thus saith the Lord." II Timothy 3:16 says that the written word, the Bible, is for doctrine, reproof, correction, and instruction. Spoken prophecy does not hold the same weight as the written word. This is why the Word commands prophecy to be judged. This is most helpful as it helps the group determine the full extent of what God is saying in the prophecy and what is the appropriate response.

Developing the Gift of Prophecy

The person who exercises these gifts must be allowed to develop them. First attempts may be halting and imperfect. There is such a thing as developing "fluency" in the spoken gifts and, for that matter, all the other gifts as well.

Prophecy originates in the mind of God and comes to you by the Holy Spirit. However, before it can get to the people, that word must pass through your spirit and mind and your personality in order for you to give it voice. Remember that the Holy Spirit is gentle. He will never force you to say or do anything against your will. It is never proper to abruptly disrupt a service with the excuse, "I couldn't help myself."

I Corinthians 14:32 *And the spirits of the prophets are subject to the prophets.*

As you yield to the inward urge or prompting to speak a phrase or sentence, you must draw that word through your heart and mind. When that prophecy passes from the Holy Spirit, through your spirit to the congregation, interesting changes take place.

The most common effect of the human personality on a prophetic word is that it becomes laced with the Elizabethan language of the King James Bible. This points up that it is possible for a word to become garbled by your attitude, experiences, and spiritual maturity. A bad attitude or unforgiveness causes a word meant to edify to actually beat down and discourage a group. Phrases like, "Do you not know . . .

?" or "Have you not heard . . . ?" often indicate such a garbled prophecy. Other phrases like, "Little children, look unto me . . . " should be watched very carefully. They can indicate a person's prophesying out of a need for attention rather than the Spirit's leading.

Remember that these human accents on prophetic words are a natural part of the learning process of maturing into the gifts. You should not be embarrassed or offended by giving or receiving these kinds of words. These accents can even at times be desirable. But we should all be ready to receive correction and guidance in stride to attain to the pure word of the Lord.

I Corinthians 14:39 *Wherefore, brethren, covet to prophesy, and forbid not to speak with tongues.*

Judging Prophecy

I Corinthians 14:29 *Let the prophets speak two or three, and let the other judge.*

All prophecy should be judged and examined. The criteria are that it lines up with the written word of God. It should be accurate to the circumstances and situations it addresses. Its tone should be uplifting to the individual or group and glorify the name of Jesus.

It is a leader's place at times to provoke you to prophesy when you have not shown the ability to share God's word with a group. Do not be intimidated by this or by an instruction to hold a prophecy to a group or individual until a proper time. The prophetic gifts are subject to the authority of the elders in the church. Prophecy is an exciting gift in which to operate. Do not hold back another day in allowing God to use you in this powerful gift.

Tongues and Interpretation

God is a god who speaks. He created the worlds with His words, and He communicated verbally with Adam and Eve in the dawn of creation. He spoke to Noah regarding the Ark and the judgment of the world. He conversed with His men and women in all ages and dispensations.

God is not quiet, shy, or introverted. He has provided many ways that we may communicate with Him--primarily in His Word, the Bible. God also speaks to us by His inward presences in our minds and consciences, further through chosen teachers and proclaimers, and additionally through the present-day gifts of utterance (including tongues and interpretation).

What Are Tongues?

Tongues (see Acts 2:1-4; I Co. 12:10) are defined as "Spirit-inspired speaking in which the conscious mind plays no part." It is the speaking of a language (known or angelic) unlearned by the speaker.

Interpretation is the God-given inspiration to speak in a known tongue the equivalent or sense of that which is spoken in unknown tongues. An interpretation is not a translation. This is why a lengthy tongue can have a very brief interpretation.

Two Gifts Working Together

Tongues and interpretation are two sides of the same coin. Paul could not conceive on one without the other. These two gifts together are the equivalent of prophecy. When a tongue is given, it is proper to expect interpretation, particularly if a tongue is addressed publicly before a group. Commonly, the teaching is that there are different kinds of tongues. This is not held up in Scripture. There is one gift of tongues for all purposes and any may be interpreted whether tongues are spoken in personal prayer times or in open meetings.

The Benefit of Tongues and Interpretation

Tongues and interpretation facilitate praise to God. They operate in prayer and have the same purpose as prophecy in public meetings. Jude 20 teaches that they build one up in his faith and spiritual character. Tongues are an excellent way of giving thanks.

I Corinthians 14:17 *For thou verily givest thanks well, but the other is not edified.*

Tongues can also be used by God to win the unbeliever.

I Corinthians 14:22 *Wherefore tongues are for a sign, not to them that believe, but to them that believe not.*

A Place to Begin

Tongues were the base-line gift that God gave in Acts 2:1-4 to inaugurate the early church into the powerful dynamics of the operation of the gifts of the Spirit in their daily lives. Tongues are not to be strived for or fretted over. As a Spirit-born believer, you can now speak in tongues. Depending on you and the Lord, the first time you open to the Lord in this area can be a fantastic experience or a very quiet experience.

A good beginning is to have quiet times in prayer before God as they did in Acts 2:1-4. During that time there were utterances presented to their minds they then verbalized. This yielding to the Spirit brought on a tremendous emotional release and a deep sense of rapture. There was also an outburst of signs and wonders such as the earthquake near the room where they were praying. The experience may be very quiet for you, but the important thing is to wait upon the Lord and take the utterance that comes to your heart as a gift from Him and speak it. Then take that capacity and, at will, exercise it when in need of strength or prompted by the Spirit to do so.

Chapter Thirty-Eight: The Motivational Gifts

There are seven gifts mentioned in Romans 12:6-8 that have come to be referred to as the motivational gifts. These differ from the leadership gifts and the nine ministry gifts. These gifts involve divinely-imbedded character traits that God has sown into the personality of every believer. Each believer's motive gift manifests itself as a drive or (as some may prefer) a calling. They shape each believer's personality and serve to mold him or her into the body of Christ as a living member, rather than merely a spectator in an audience.

The motivational gifts are important because God does not want us to do some "cold" service for Him. He wants us to be driven to do a work for Him because the passion for this work is in us. We see some members of the church who have great zeal for God, and they passionately embrace their work for the Lord. Why? Are they more spiritual? Not necessarily. They only recognized their motivational gift and are allowed to accomplish that gift; that is, to motivate, get one excited, and be encouraged to work for Jesus.

Again, every believer is endowed with some motive gift. The different gifts are prophecy, serving, teaching, exhortation, giving, ruling, and mercy. God has a work for you, and He has put a gift inside you that drives you to want to do this work.

A further purpose of the motivation gifts is for you to discover who you are in the body of Christ. Jesus does not want you to look like someone else but wants you to be you. He does not want the hand to imitate the foot or the foot to imitate the ear. As you discover your motivational gift, you will discover who you are in the body of Christ, and soon you will be doing the things God has called you (not because you have to but because you want to).

A motive gift is a supernatural drive implanted in you to motivate you to service for the Lord. It has often been said that the combined motive gifts make up the personality of God in the church.

You will see yourself often in all the gifts because Jesus lives in you and all gifts are a part of Him. Yet, there will be one gift that remarkably fits your personality. As you read the description of each gift, you will see some traits that best fit you. You will begin to locate yourself spiritually in the body of Christ. You will also recognize the gifts of others. Rather than get caught up in misunderstanding and offense because they are not more like you and see things your way, understanding another man's gift will enable you to walk more in harmony with the whole body.

The Motivational Gift of Prophecy

The first motive gift listed in Romans 12 is the gift of prophecy. Even if you have never prophesied in a public meeting, you can still have this motive gift of prophecy. Also, because you may have this motive gift of prophecy does not qualify you to become a prophet. We are not talking about ministry offices but your sincere motives. More important than your function in the church is the motive behind that function. It must flow out of a genuine response to fulfilling your personal destiny in God.

The person who has the motive gift of prophecy tends to have the ability to discern peoples' characters and motives. He is introspective, he is a self-examiner looking deep within his own intentions. He is often too hard on himself. He is quick to judge sin in his own life, and he grows to hate sin. He equally hates the sin he sees in others. He wants sin exposed in his own life and also in others. He is very quick to identify sin and point the finger at it.

After all the introspection and mediation upon how God hates sin, a message wells up within the prophecy-motivated person and must come forth. The person who has this gift is one who must speak forth the message God is burning within him. This message comes out with authority and conviction because he sincerely means what he says. He sees sin as God sees it. He sees the seriousness and need for repentance.

This person affects those around him by bringing conviction into their lives. He desires to see an evidence of people moved to change. If you are motivated by the gift, you want to see fruit in an individual's life. A prophecy-motivated individual hates sin but loves the sinner. He will come down hard and will sometimes be misunderstood by others. He is accused of being harsh, callous, and intolerant.

The person with this gifting can be so burdened by his message and his need to get it out that he gives the appearance of not being interested in anyone else. He has the unique ability to look at the body as a whole. He is interested in groups. He is very concerned for the reputation of the church. He is often a loner. Because of his boldness and conviction, he often repels close friendships. Not everyone wants to be around the person who is prone to meteoric shifts in demeanor and intensity such as the prophecy-motivated individual. This motivational gift can be symbolized by the pointed finger. Is that you? Are you driven inside with such a hatred for second best that you must expose compromise in a verbal way? Maybe you know someone who is like that, or maybe you are not like that at all.

The complement to the gift of prophecy is the gift of mercy. These are two extremes, and God is in both. He hates sin and compromise. He requires repentance and change. He also moves in great mercy toward those in failure, loving them to the turning point in their lives where they forsake worldliness and fully come to him.

The Gift of Mercy

These people are very sensitive individuals. They can walk into a room and read the atmosphere like a newspaper headline. They are quick to pick up when someone is depressed, hurt, dejected, rejected, joyous, happy, etc. They are very sensitive to others' moods even when they are masked.

Mercy-motivated people are drawn to the underdog. They are attracted to people who are hurting. They literally take on the feeling of the one hurting as if it were himself or herself. They must be careful to exercise their gift cheerfully. If not careful, the mercy-motivated person will take on the offense of others and become bitter. These people desire to bring healing to those that are hurting inside by displaying the genuine tenderness, compassion, understanding, and forgiveness of Jesus.

The Gift of Serving

It is very unnatural for man to want to serve. It is in our nature to desire to be served instead. We are naturally proud, thinking we deserve service. Service is truly a godly quality. Jesus came not to be served but to serve. In the manifestation of the motive of serving, we see Jesus as the humble servant.

A person motivated with this gift is usually very down-to-earth (his head is not in the clouds). This person is so practical that others often misjudge him or her as being unspiritual. This individual is also very observant. A good servant sees immediate needs and tends to them right away. He notices if the church is clean, if the chairs are straight, if there is toilet paper in the bathroom. They notice if people wear the same clothes over and over. Some people think they are nosy, but they are actually driven by this gift to meet practical needs. They look for needs and are concerned about the comfort of others.

Chapter Thirty-nine: Motivational Gifts (continued)

The Gift of Ruling

Ruling means "one who stands in front of others." In this gift we see Jesus expressing His leadership qualities through the personalities of members of the body of Christ. These people are the eyes of the church.

- They see what needs to be done.
- They see what they have to work with.
- They are realists.
- They see problems, assets, failures, victories, etc.
- They see potential in other members and co-workers.
- They are goal setters and set goals for themselves and others.
- They are very conscious of time and figures.
- They are extremely faithful once they commit themselves. They are like one who commits to put together a 5000-piece jigsaw puzzle. They know it takes time and clear thinking and are not so foolish as to become exhausted trying to piece the entire picture together in one night.

This individual operates by the numbers--step one, step two, step three, etc. People sometimes see him or her as slow and unyielding because of a lack of patience. They want to see step three before step one and two are ever undertaken. An organizer or ruler clearly formulates in his or her mind the steps of action to meet goals.

Unlike the server, a ruler does not like to work alone. This person has long-range vision. Therefore, he sees many jobs and knows there is enough for everybody. He sees the futility in working alone, is good at delegating authority, and is very good at finding those that are a suitable fit for a particular job. Because he often delegates authority, some misjudge him as lazy and sitting on the sidelines while others are out working.

The ruler is motivated to make things as easy as possible for co-workers. He or she makes sure they have the necessary equipment, enough help, etc. These people are not easily discouraged, and their vision encourages them. They are not procrastinators, and neither do they rush into things. They have a mind to work. Because of their eagerness to see goals met, people often think they are more concerned with the program than the people. Their joy comes when they see the pieces of their puzzle (or vision) come together. They have a great desire for unity. The puzzle is not complete until every piece is in place.

As we look at creation and view the prophecies in the Old Testament, we can see the organization of our Lord. Long before you were born, He devised a plan of which you and I are now a part. The ruling gift is God's tool to continually shape our efforts to further that plan.

The Gift of Teaching

A person with a motivation for teaching demonstrates Jesus as the way and the truth. He is concerned with truth. He is driven by an intense desire to know and communicate truth. He has a strong attraction and commitment to the Word of God. He views the Bible as truth and has a strong desire to study it. This gift brings a real reverence for the Word, and he will never take a verse out of context to prove a point and is very disappointed when someone else does this very thing. He has a unique ability to see the interweaving of God's Word from one chapter to the next.

Teachers with this motivational gift are teachable themselves. They hunger and thirst for truth. They are excited when they hear the Word and soak it up like a sponge. Yet, they totally reject what they perceive as false doctrine and will go to great lengths to expose it. They realize that without a clear understanding of the Word that man can and will be deceived. They are motivated to teach to the ignorance they see in man.

Motivational teachers break down Scripture and are careful to give accurate interpretation to words by looking them up in the original languages. They desire to see minds renewed. They present their message logically, systematically, clearly, and repetitively. They use a lot of Scripture because it is God's Word they want to get across and not just an opinion.

In wanting to be accurate, teachers sometimes share unnecessary details (all the while the listener is hoping there is a point to all this detail). But, the teaching motivator wants the truth to be firmly grasped. Because of the impossibility of exhausting the Word, they tend to stay on one subject too long and miss the Holy Spirit's new direction. They never lack a message, and they are never empty but always full of the Word. They are meditators of the Word. The prophecy motivator speaks to the heart, whereas the teaching motivator speaks to the mind.

<u>The Gift of Exhortation</u>

The exhorter is an encourager--a true evangelist. Somewhat like a coach or cheerleader, he is very paternal and reassuring. He is on the sideline telling you, "You can do all things through Christ, who strengthens you." He does not like to see people discouraged. He is positive and well-liked among the people.

A true evangelist sees the positive process of God in all things. He often misunderstands the benefits of chastisement, yet he learns through experience, both good and bad. In helping others he relies on his experiences (a teacher would never do this) which he backs with the Word. The exhorter will give a step-by-step account of how the Lord took him through a process; that is, how they share the Word. Experiences are very real to an evangelist, and he relives them over and again, deriving more benefit each time. He has the ability to see God in all circumstances, and when no one else can, he sees light in darkness.

An exhorter is a lifestyle evangelist and firmly believes that actions speak louder than words. He has the ability not to judge others but to accept them as they are. He is quick to take someone who needs encouragement under his wing. He is the backslider's best friend. Exhorters defend people, whereas, the teacher defends the Word. He or she loves people and makes a good counselor. Unlike the teacher, an evangelist will use Scripture out of context to prove a point.

The exhorter is a picture of God the Father, a mighty exhorter, who left us a cloud of witnesses who successfully walked the walk of faith. He encourages us through the lives of great men of God and the faith walk of Jesus.

The Gift of Giving

This gift truly reveals the heart of God. God so loved that He "gave." The person with this motive gift is driven to give of his money, time, and resources. He sees the need, and it stirs up his desire to give. He will always give his best. He gives without hesitation and seldom considers his own needs first. These people give unconditionally versus some offerings that are not gifts but bribes to hear what someone wants to hear. A person with the motive gift of giving gives freely with no strings attached, no manipulation, and no deals.

John 3:26 *For God so loved the world, that he gave his only begotten Son, that whosoever believeth in him should not perish, but have everlasting life.*

God gave His Son unconditionally that whosoever would believe in Him would have everlasting life. God would have given Jesus even if no man would have appreciated the gift and received Him as Savior.

A giver never misses a tithe for any reason. They are wise spenders, and they make good businessmen. They are not gullible. They get more for the dollar and, in essence, are generally financially blessed although they may not live like it. They are not inclined to spend on themselves but save in order to give more.

Givers are volunteers; they are the support team of the church. They support the ministry with money, prayer, time, and energy. They have a strong desire to spread the Gospel. They will generally ask God for a specific amount to give and will only give what they hear God tell them to give. They are quiet givers and are angered by those who let their right hand know what their left is doing. Their greatest delight is to discover their gift was a direct answer to prayer.

What Is Your Gift?

God's desire is that we all learn from each other. You should be a role model in the gift that you seem to possess so that others can learn from you; freely give out what you have. In turn, be a learner and do not be satisfied with your gift alone. If we do not learn from others, sooner or later we are going to find ourselves fighting and running from the will of God because of the harness of our hearts toward one another. In order for the body of Christ to be balanced, we must learn from one another (it is not an option). We must lay aside all personality conflicts and purpose to see Jesus in each other. It is time to join together and grow together into His purpose for us as a people.

Chapter Forty: The End Times (Part 1)

This course would be incomplete without a discussion of the end times. This important aspect of the Christian life deals with the coming of the Lord to visibly set up His kingdom in the earth. This involves a series of future events predicted by the Bible prophets concerning God's intervention in the affairs of man as He draws human existence (as we have known it) to a close. He will then initiate an open, visible reign over the earth for all eternity. Evil will no longer exist, and there will be no more death, tears, or sorrow. The throne of God, now spiritually located in heaven, will be geographically located here on earth.

These plans are found in prophetic predictions that have proven themselves already with pinpoint accuracy concerning world events that have occurred since God spoke with Daniel. These forecasts may seem Utopian and outside the realm of possibility, but the Scriptures in their inerrancy and inspiration point to a cataclysmic series of events in the "end times" which will culminate in the emergence of a visible government of God over all the earth for time without end.

Since the days of the Apostles, men have believed they were living at the end of time. More and more as we study Scriptures and look at prophecies that have been fulfilled and other prophecies that read like today's headlines, we are compelled to believe that the last series of events leading to the “visible kingdom” are immediately upon us.

In any study of the end times, most people begin with the book of Revelation. This book, however, deals mostly with events that have yet to come to pass and address these matters in symbolic language that make little sense without some frame of reference.

The book of Daniel gives a time reference for most major aspects of Bible prophecy. There are two reasons for this: (1) Many of the prophecies in Daniel have already come to pass; and, (2) Daniel contains prophecies that give a general overview of God's plan of the ages that is concise, comprehensive, and very easy to understand.

The Prophet Daniel

Daniel was a Judaic captive who served as an advisor to rulers in the Babylonian and Persian Empire. His life story is remarkable reading in itself, recording the supernatural dealings through which he and his companions were promoted from slavery to the highest echelons of world power.

During the course of his life, Daniel received several visions that pointed to our times. The first consideration, however, is a dream he interpreted for Nebuchadnezzar found in Chapter 2 of Daniel. The king did not tell anyone what the dream meant, but Daniel prayed, and the Lord revealed the dream as well as its interpretation to him.

Daniel 2:27-29 *Daniel answered in the presence of the king, and said, The secret which the king hath demanded cannot the wise [men], the astrologers, the magicians, the soothsayers, shew unto the king; (v. 28) But there is a God in heaven that revealeth secrets, and maketh known to the king Nebuchadnezzar what shall be in the latter days. Thy dream, and the visions of thy head upon thy bed, are these; (v.29) As for thee, O king, thy thoughts came [into thy mind] upon thy bed, what should come to pass hereafter: and he that revealeth secrets maketh known to thee what shall come to pass.*

The Importance of Dreams

King Solomon wrote in Ecclesiastes 5:3 that a dream "cometh from a multitude of business." In other words, a dream from God is usually given in the context of your most immediate concerns. In this case the king was troubled about the future of mankind and the end of the world. Therefore, God spoke to him in regard to his concerns.

Daniel 2:30-38 *But as for me, this secret is not revealed to me for [any] wisdom that I have more than any living, but for [their] sakes that shall* *make known the interpretation to the king, and that thou mightest know the thoughts of thy heart. (v. 31) Thou, O king, sawest, and behold a great image. This great image, whose brightness [was] excellent, stood before thee; and the form thereof [was] terrible. (v. 32) This image's head [was] of fine gold, his breast and his arms of silver, his belly and his thighs of brass, (v. 33) His legs of iron, his feet part of iron and part of clay. (v. 34) Thou sawest till that a stone was cut out without hands, which smote the image upon his feet [that were] of iron and clay, and brake them to pieces. (v. 35) Then was the iron, the clay, the brass, the silver, and the gold, broken to pieces together, and became like the chaff of the summer threshingfloors; and the wind carried them away, that no place was found for them: and the stone that smote the image became a great mountain, and filled the whole earth. (v. 36) This [is] the dream; and we will tell the interpretation thereof before the king. (v. 37) Thou, O king, [art] a king of kings: for the God of heaven hath given thee a kingdom, power, and strength, and glory. (v. 38) And wheresoever the children of men dwell, the beasts of the field and the fowls of the heaven hath he given into thine hand, and hath made thee ruler over them all. Thou [art] this head of gold.*

The King's Dream of the Kingdoms of the Earth

Here we find a frame of reference for this image in the king's dream. King Nebuchadnezzar is the ruler of a world power at this time. The image then is speaking of the progression through time of the governments of men and what their end will be from the period of Nebuchadnezzar's reign. Nebuchadnezzar and the kingdom of Babylon are represented by the head of gold. Later on, the king (in his vanity) erected an entire image of gold and commanded men to worship it. This is an example of how the wisdom of God is lost on the minds of men.

Daniel 2:39 *And after thee shall arise another kingdom inferior to thee, and another third kingdom of brass, which shall bear rule over all the earth.*

The next kingdom that arose after Babylon was the kingdom of the Medes and the Persians. They are represented by the breast and arms of silver. The third kingdom was the kingdom of Alexander the Great.

Daniel 2:40 *And the fourth kingdom shall be strong as iron: forasmuch as iron breaketh in pieces and subdueth all [things]: and as iron that breaketh all these, shall it break in pieces and bruise.*

The fourth kingdom was the Roman Empire signified here in two parts: (1) The ancient Roman kingdom symbolized by the legs of iron; and (2) the aspect of the Roman Empire denoted in the next four verses.

Daniel 2:41-43 *And whereas thou sawest the feet and toes, part of potters' clay, and part of iron, the kingdom shall be divided; but there shall be in it of the strength of the iron, forasmuch as thou sawest the iron mixed with miry clay. (v. 42) And [as] the toes of the feet [were] part of iron, and part of clay, [so] the kingdom shall be partly strong, and partly broken. (v. 43) And whereas thou sawest iron mixed with miry clay, they shall mingle themselves with the seed of men: but they shall not cleave one to another, even as iron is not mixed with clay.*

What these verses describe is that after the "iron legs" part of the Roman Empire shifts (what historians call the fall of the Roman Empire), there will be a continuation of it symbolized by the feet and toes of iron and clay. Remember, the dream is speaking of governments. The feet and toes suggest a loose confederation of nations that will develop out of the remnants of the ancient Roman Empire.

Daniel 2:44 *And in the days of these kings shall the God of heaven set up a kingdom, which shall never be destroyed: and the kingdom shall not be left to other people, [but] it shall break in pieces and consume all these kingdoms, and it shall stand for ever.*

<u>We Are Living in the Last Days</u>

At the time of the "iron and clay" kingdoms, the Lord speaks of setting up His eternal kingdom that will subdue all human rule and power under itself.

Daniel 2:45 *Forasmuch as thou sawest that the stone was cut out of the mountain without hands, and that it brake in pieces the iron, the brass, the clay, the silver, and the gold; the great God hath made known to the king what shall come to pass hereafter: and the dream [is] certain, and the interpretation thereof sure.*

The Scriptures reveal Jesus as "the stone that the builders rejected." Mountains in the Bible represent powers and in this case the "mountain of the Lord." This verse then predicts Jesus coming in power to destroy human government and society as we know it and establishing His visible kingdom in the earth. This one dream gives the most basic understanding of God's plan for the ages to be found in the Scriptures.

Now we can easily place ourselves in the unfolding of this revelation. The present day is located in this interpretation between the "legs of iron" and the "feet and toes of iron and clay." We are in the time when the Roman Empire has changed from a solid, dominate world government. Yet out of its abeyance, there is beginning to emerge in Europe and the Mediterranean a new solidarity and fledging spirit of cooperation known as the E. C. (European Community) or the European Common Market. The E. C., incidentally, has 12 members, but 2 of the members opted out in the summer of 1992 and then swayed back in. Interestingly, the 10 members reveal themselves as the "10 toes" of iron and clay.

It can be seen plainly then from the Scriptures that we are indeed living in the last days. The final expression of human government, the E. C., is in the final stages of development. In the aftermath of the fall of the Soviet Union, the E. C. is moving swiftly toward a common currency and defense as a new "United States of Europe." This will be *the* superpower to watch in the next ten years as the U. S. returns to its traditional protectionism in hopes of resolving its economic problems.

When it solidifies into a superpower, this emerging world government will set the stage for the Son of God to come in judgment and destruction and will sweep away the government of man and establish the visible government of God in the earth.

Chapter Forty-one: The End Times (Part 2)

Now we move to the next vision of the end times in Daniel for more insight regarding the end times. There is much repetition in these visions and dreams, each showing a different perspective. Studying prophecy can be compared to peeling an onion. Each layer reveals other layers beneath it.

The Vision of the Four Beasts

Daniel 7:1 *In the first year of Belshazzar king of Babylon Daniel had a dream and visions of his head upon his bed: then he wrote the dream, [and] told the sum of the matters.*

Daniel's dream in Chapter 7 deals with events that have since come to pass. These prophecies give a unique opportunity to observe how transpiring events are described in prophetic revelations.

When interpreting prophecy of future events and discerning how the poetic language applies to current events, you must hold your predictions loosely. They may not pan out like your first reading of them might indicate. Many Christians make shipwrecks of their lives by dogmatic assertions on dates, times, and events they thought the Scriptures clearly revealed. There are events which seem clear and time frames that clearly suggest themselves. However, if these viewpoints do not materialize, then you must let them go and return to the Scriptures for greater light and understanding. With this in mind you can go with an open mind to the prophets and allow them to suggest to us the immediacy of the days in which we live.

Daniel 7:2-3 *Daniel spake and said, I saw in my vision by night, and, behold, the four winds of the heaven strove upon the great sea. (v. 3) And four great beasts came up from the sea, diverse one from another.*

These four beasts correspond to the four aspects of the image in the king's dream previously discussed. Again, the Lord is revealing a prophetic time line. Read the dream and then move to the verses where an angel interprets Daniel's dream to him.

Daniel 7:4 *The first [was] like a lion, and had eagle's wings: I beheld till the wings thereof were plucked, and it was lifted up from the earth, and made stand upon the feet as a man, and a man's heart was given to it.*

This is the kingdom of Babylon and corresponds to the head of gold in Nebuchadnezzar's dream. The heart of a man being given to it was fulfilled in God's dealings with the king in Daniel Chapter 4 when he was humbled before the Lord because of his pride and confessed openly his submission to the God of the Hebrews.

Daniel 7:5 *And behold another beast, a second, like to a bear, and it raised up itself on one side, and [it had] three ribs in the mouth of it between the teeth of it: and they said thus unto it, Arise, devour much flesh.*

This second kingdom is the Persian and Median world power that was about to overthrow Babylon at the time of this dream. This corresponds to the shoulders of silver in the king's dream.

Daniel 7:6 *After this I beheld, and lo another, like a leopard, which had upon the back of it four wings of a fowl; the beast had also four heads; and dominion was given to it.*

This next world dominion is that of Alexander the Great. The four wings of the leopard symbolize the four generals to whom Alexander's kingdom was divided at the time of his death. This corresponds to the belly of brass in the king's dream.

Daniel 7:7 *After this I saw in the night visions, and behold a fourth beast, dreadful and terrible, and strong exceedingly; and it had great iron teeth: it devoured and brake in pieces, and stamped the residue with the feet of it: and it [was] diverse from all the beasts that [were] before it; and it had ten horns.*

This fourth beast is the Roman Empire and corresponds to the legs of iron and feet and toes of iron and clay. Notice that it is represented in two aspects just as it was in the king's dream. First, the verse above identifies the Roman Empire in its glory. Caesar ruled the known world with an iron hand across a diverse empire embracing Africa, the Middle East, Europe, and Central Asia.

The second aspect of this vision that does not fit ancient Rome is the "ten horns." Horns in the Scriptures represent powers or governments. These ten horns correspond to the ten toes of iron and clay in the king's dream. It is important to see these ten horns as an aspect of the Roman Empire. In the modern perspective, the Roman Empire is no more. But from God's perspective, it has not simply fallen but has gone into abeyance or dormancy only to reemerge in a different manifestation typified by the ten horns.

Daniel 7:8 *I considered the horns, and, behold, there came up among them another little horn, before whom there were three of the first horns plucked up by the roots: and, behold, in this horn [were] eyes like the eyes of man, and a mouth speaking great things.*

With the exception of the second aspect of the Roman Empire coming out of abeyance and attaining the status of a super power, verses two through seven have already come to pass. Looking at the current situation in world politics, the E. C. (European Community) most aptly fits the description of the ten horns. They comprise a confederacy of approximately ten nations located in the same geographical location as ancient Rome.

The horn with eyes and a mouth speaks not simply of a government but of a leader--a leader who apparently will bring three of the horns or governments in the ten-nation confederacy into one government under himself. This would have seemed impossible ten years ago, but given the political climate in Europe after the reunification of Germany, this is not at all improbable.

Daniel 7:9 *I beheld till the thrones were cast down, and the Ancient of* *days did sit, whose garment [was] white as snow, and the hair of his head like the pure wool: his throne [was like] the fiery flame, [and] his wheels [as] burning fire.*

This verse would clearly correspond to the king's dream, where the rock (Jesus) crushes the image. This is the appearance of Jesus on the world scene, changing His role from Shepherd/Redeemer to Righteous Judge.

The point to ponder here is the phrase, "I beheld till the thrones were cast down . . . ." The better rendering is, "Till the thrones were put in place . . . ." The mention of these thrones being put in place are the ten horns or ten toes representing the ten powers or governments arising out of the ancient Roman Empire.

The world events which most clearly fit this scenario are those surrounding the European Community (the E. C., Common Market, or European United States). As of this writing, the E. C. has 12 members. Prophecy indicates a ten-member confederacy. Interesting enough, Britain and Germany opted in and out of economic ties with the E. C. in 1992. This shows that their allegiance could finally be placed outside the E. C., leaving it with ten members. Thus, the "thrones would be in place" for the appearance of the Messiah/Judge.

Daniel 7:10-11 *A fiery stream issued and came forth from before him (returned Messiah): thousand thousands ministered unto him, and ten thousand times ten thousand stood before him: the judgment was set, and the books were opened. (v. 11) I beheld then because of the voice of the great words which the horn (E. C. leader of three unified nations) spake: I beheld [even] till the beast was slain, and his body destroyed, and given to the burning flame.*

The Kingdom of God begins to emerge as a visible strength in the world at this time. Simultaneously, the little horn (an aggressive leader in the E. C. and head of state over three newly unified European states) will overstep himself and be slain. Whether at the hands of

Christ himself or under other circumstances, it is not clear here how he dies. Revelation does speak of the "Anti-Christ" being thrown into a lake of fire at the inception of a thousand-year reign of the visible government of God.

Daniel 7:12 *As concerning the rest of the beasts, they had their dominion taken away: yet their lives were prolonged for a season and time.*

The prolongation of other world governments under the reign of Christ would bear out Revelation's teachings that national borders will continue during what is known as the millennial or thousand-year reign of Christ.

Daniel 7:13-14 *I saw in the night visions, and, behold, [one] like the Son of man came with the clouds of heaven, and came to the Ancient of days, and they brought him near before him. (v. 14) And there was given him dominion, and glory, and a kingdom, that all people, nations, and languages, should serve him: his dominion [is] an everlasting dominion, which shall not pass away, and his kingdom [that] which shall not be destroyed.*

This is clearly the final disposition of human history as we have known it. The events leading up to this time are yet to be fulfilled and involve the reemergence of a European superpower (which seems to answer to the E. C.) and the unification of three European states under a charismatic Gorbachev-type leader. And, this leader's destruction is subsequent to the all-out takeover of world government by Jesus Christ with the saints.

Chapter Forty-two: The End Times (Part 3)

Daniel has had a dream about the rise and fall of four superpowers that culminated with the visible reign of Jesus Christ as Messiah King. He did not understand the vision, and in time an angel comes to interpret it for him.

The Reemergence of the Roman Empire in Modern Times

Daniel 7:15-16 *I Daniel was grieved in my spirit in the midst of [my] body, and the visions of my head troubled me. (v. 16) I came near unto one of them that stood by, and asked him the truth of all this. So he told me, and made me know the interpretation of the things.*

During an angelic visitation, Daniel is made to understand the vision. Interestingly, the angel interprets hundreds of years of history from Babylon to ancient Rome in two verses. There is then much explanation put into the understanding of the last and most terrible human government yet to come.

Daniel 7:17-18 *These great beasts, which are four, [are] four kings, [which] shall arise out of the earth. (v. 18) But the saints of the most High shall take the kingdom, and possess the kingdom for ever, even for ever and ever.*

If you need an eschatology (study of the end things), this is it in a nutshell. Human government will be in manifestation through four great world powers, and then the saints of God will overwhelm and conquer, establishing the eternal government of God.

Daniel 7:19 *Then I would know the truth of the fourth beast, which was diverse from all the others, exceeding dreadful, whose teeth [were of] iron, and his nails [of] brass; [which] devoured, brake in pieces, and stamped the residue with his feet.*

The verse above was fulfilled in the emergence and downfall of the ancient Roman Empire.

Daniel 7:20 *And of the ten horns that [were] in his head, and [of] the other which came up, and before whom three fell; even [of] that horn that had eyes, and a mouth that spake very great things, whose look [was] more stout than his fellows.*

This verse describes a federation of ten powers or governments that come out of the head of the ancient Roman Empire. (It is necessary to note at this point that [of the Roman Empire] its headship is the only thing that has lasted to our day.)

Constantine, one of the last emperors of Rome, merged the secular office of emperor with the religious office of pope or head of the church. Therefore, the headship of the ancient Roman Empire is with us today. In that sense it can be understood how God represents the Roman Empire as never "falling" but going into abeyance and reemerging as a world power at a later time. These events are forming even as you read this writing.

Daniel 7:21 *I beheld, and the same horn made war with the saints, and prevailed against them.*

The horn mentioned here is apparently the flag ship government of the European Community or Common Market. It will consist of three European nations unified under a charismatic leader. It can be expected that this leader will be either an atheist or perhaps a religious zealot like Paul was before his conversion. In any case he will vigorously oppose true Christianity even as Hitler opposed the Jews.

Daniel 7:22 *Until the Ancient of days came, and judgment was given to the saints of the most High; and the time came that the saints possessed the kingdom.*

This leader is successful in his tactics of oppression and persecution against true Christianity until Jesus comes and with the saints brings judgment and overthrows his power.

Daniel 7:23 *Thus he said, The fourth beast shall be the fourth kingdom* *upon earth, which shall be diverse from all kingdoms, and shall devour the whole earth, and shall tread it down, and break it in pieces.*

This again is the first aspect of the fourth beast or world power that was fulfilled by ancient Rome.

Daniel 7:24 *And the ten horns out of this kingdom [are] ten kings [that] shall arise: and another shall rise after them; and he shall be diverse from the first, and he shall subdue three kings.*

This ten-member confederation, which is most like the European Community (E. C.), will arise out of the historic background of the Roman Empire. They will have stronger ties to the Vatican than other European states. Out of this confederation will emerge three nations unified through the leadership of a charismatic, aggressive leader under one flag.

Daniel 7:25 *And he shall speak [great] words against the most High, and shall wear out the saints of the most High, and think to change times and laws: and they shall be given into his hand until a time and times and the dividing of time.*

This leader will have an ambitious reform agenda and will no doubt brand Christianity as outmoded and having no place in the New World Order. He will bring legal reform and no doubt introduce broad changes in weights and measures (somewhat like the introduction of the metric system, etc.).

Daniel 7:26 *But the judgment shall sit, and they shall take away his dominion, to consume and to destroy [it] unto the end.*

Notice that the "they" here are the saints of God. In spite of his efforts to destroy and weaken Christianity, it will be empowered to overwhelm and conquer this world power.

Daniel 7:27 *And the kingdom and dominion, and the greatness of the kingdom under the whole heaven, shall be given to the people of the* *saints of the most High, whose kingdom [is] an everlasting kingdom, and all dominions shall serve and obey him.*

The destruction of this world power will result in all the kingdoms of the earth coming under some form of theocratic rule administered by the empowered believers who participate with Jesus in the overthrow of this government.

Chapter Forty-three: The End Times (Part 4)

Let us go on to the next vision in Daniel. You will notice there is considerable repetition. We reproduce the same here because it facilitates the revealing of different facets of the same events.

<u>The Vision of the Ram and the Goat: The Fall of Babylon to the Reemergence of the Roman Empire</u>

Daniel 8:1-3 *In the third year of the reign of king Belshazzar a vision appeared unto me, [even unto] me Daniel, after that which appeared unto me at the first. (v. 2) And I saw in a vision; and it came to pass, when I saw, that I [was] at Shushan [in] the palace, which [is] in the province of Elam; and I saw in a vision, and I was by the river of Ulai. (v. 3) Then I lifted up mine eyes, and saw, and, behold, there stood before the river a ram which had [two] horns: and the [two] horns [were] high; but one [was] higher than the other, and the higher came up last.*

Now, let us look at how the angel interprets the vision as Daniel experienced it. The context of the vision is as follows:

Daniel 8:17 *. . . Understand, O son of man: for at the time of the end [shall] be the vision.*

Daniel 8:19-20 *. . . I will make thee know what shall be in the last end of the indignation: for at the time appointed the end [shall be]. (v. 20) The ram which thou sawest having [two] horns [are] the kings of Media and Persia.*

This first part of verse three has already come to pass. The ram with two horns represent the Medes and Persians who are in power at the time Daniel has this vision.

Daniel 8:4 *I saw the ram pushing westward, and northward, and southward; so that no beasts might stand before him, neither [was there* *any] that could deliver out of his hand; but he did according to his will, and became great.*

This verse is foretelling to Daniel the successful domination of the known world by the Medes and Persians. But the next verse describes the fall of this empire which, obviously, has also been fulfilled.

Daniel 8:5 *And as I was considering, behold, an he goat came from the west on the face of the whole earth, and touched not the ground: and the goat [had] a notable horn between his eyes.*

This goat is a type pointing to Alexander the Great. The horn between his eyes represents his great power, which surpassed all others before it in regard to lands conquered in the shortest period of time.

Daniel 8:6-7 *And he came to the ram that had [two] horns, which I had seen standing before the river, and ran unto him in the fury of his power. (v. 7) And I saw him come close unto the ram, and he was moved with choler against him, and smote the ram, and brake his two horns: and there was no power in the ram to stand before him, but he cast him down to the ground, and stamped upon him: and there was none that could deliver the ram out of his hand.*

These verses describe the manner in which Alexander the Great overthrew the Persian Empire.

Daniel 8:8 *Therefore the he goat waxed very great: and when he was strong, the great horn was broken; and for it came up four notable ones toward the four winds of heaven.*

In the height of his conquest, Alexander the Great was cut down. No heir to his throne was left. Therefore, his great power (the one horn) was broken up and divided between four of his military leaders (the great horn becoming four notable ones). It is amazing to read this account and realize that while none of this had occurred at that time that these predictions were fulfilled to the letter by ensuing world events. This is what the Angel Gabriel explained to Daniel when he gave the interpretation.

Daniel 8:21-22 *And the rough goat [is] the king of Grecia: and the great horn that [is] between his eyes [is] the first king. (v. 22) Now that being broken, whereas four stood up for it, four kingdoms shall stand up out of the nation, but not in his power.*

Daniel 8:9 *And out of one of them came forth a little horn, which waxed exceeding great, toward the south, and toward the east, and toward the pleasant [land].*

This little horn (representing a government or power) arises out of one of the four powers established after Alexander the Great. From the four there were two significant powers. This was Ptolemy, who was established in Egypt. He is spoken of as the "Southern King." The north territory also became known as Seleucia with Alexander's general Seleucius as king. He was known as the “Northern King,” who is a foreshadowing of the Antichrist. The little horn in this verse comes out of one of the notable horns. The Seleucian kingdom eventually gave Rome access to the Mediterranean, which became the staging ground for Roman world conquest.

Verses 3 through 9 have already come to pass. Verses 10 and onward deal with the restored Roman Empire at the "appointed time" or the time of the end. These events are yet to occur. This mention of the Roman Empire does not even address the first aspect of the Roman Empire fulfilled by ancient Rome.

Daniel 8:10 *And it waxed great, [even] to the host of heaven; and it cast down [some] of the host and of the stars to the ground, and stamped upon them.*

The little horn here is the same little horn in the previous vision. This verse speaks of the time that the Antichrist comes to power over three nations in the ten-nation confederacy (most likely identified as the European Common Market). He again is a persecutor of Christianity and has designs of conquest toward Israel. The host of heaven represents the church. He apparently will deceive many in the church and bring them under his dominion.

Daniel 8:11 *Yea, he magnified [himself] even to the prince of the host, and by him the daily [sacrifice] was taken away, and the place of his sanctuary was cast down.*

Perhaps the Antichrist will deceive many in the church because he will allow himself to be thought of as a Messianic figure. He will have influence in the Middle East and close ties with Israel. The mention of the temple and daily sacrifice seems to indicate that the Jewish temple will be rebuilt, and the ancient Jewish religion will be restored.

It is commonly known that the Wailing Wall is the only remnant of the foundations of the ancient temple of the Jews. Above its ruins rests a Moslem Holy Mosque. Therefore, it would seem likely that some events will take place in Israel whereby the temple mount will be reclaimed, the Mosque destroyed, the temple rebuilt, and ancient sacrifice restored. These events would, no doubt, ignite great turmoil in the Middle East since it is unlikely the Moslem world would simply hand over the temple mount. This will be a time of great instability in Israel.

Daniel 8:12 *And an host was given [him] against the daily [sacrifice] by reason of transgression, and it cast down the truth to the ground; and it practised, and prospered.*

This Antichrist will no doubt put a stop to the temple sacrifice in order to appease the Islamic nations. He may be seeking to unify the Jewish and Islamic religions by establishing a hybrid of the two with himself as its new prophet.

Daniel 8:13-14 *Then I heard one saint speaking, and another saint said unto that certain [saint] which spake, How long [shall be] the vision [concerning] the daily [sacrifice], and the transgression of desolation, to give both the sanctuary and the host to be trodden under foot? (v. 14) And he said unto me, Unto two thousand and three hundred days; then shall the sanctuary be cleansed.*

Two thousand and three hundred (2,300) days amounts to approximately six and one-half (6½) years. The significance is unclear, but it is familiar with the seventh "tribulation" taught by many as the transitive time just before the millennial reign of Christ. Gabriel further elaborates on these future events in the following verses.

Daniel 8:23-24 *And in the latter time of their kingdom, when the transgressors are come to the full, a king of fierce countenance, and understanding dark sentences, shall stand up. (v. 24) And his power shall be mighty, but not by his own power: and he shall destroy wonderfully, and shall prosper, and practise, and shall destroy the mighty and the holy people.*

This king will have great cunning and deception. He shall rule--not by human power but rather demonic strength. He will speak peace and tranquility, but the fruits of his rule will be destruction and great persecution of the saints and the Jews.

Daniel 8:25 *And through his policy also he shall cause craft to prosper in his hand; and he shall magnify [himself] in his heart, and by peace shall destroy many: he shall also stand up against the Prince of princes; but he shall be broken without hand.*

He will bring in great commerce and initiate the economic recovery in Europe. At the time of this writing, the U. S. and Europe totter on the brink of a trade war. Farmers from all over Europe clashed in riots with police over European concessions with the U. S. These people are ignoring old prejudices and uniting in a call for reform and leadership. They are ripe for the coming of this "great king" with his dark sayings and great solutions to world problems. He will magnify himself. He will no doubt offer himself to the Catholic/Protestant/Moslem world as a new Mohammed, a Messianic figure. He will compare himself with Jesus and would succeed but for the intervention of God.

Chapter Forty-four: The End Times (Part 5)

Daniel's Understanding of the 70 Weeks: Looking to the New Millennia

Daniel was astonished and deeply troubled by what he saw. The explanation given by Gabriel gave him more questions than answers. As he waited on the Lord, he offered a great intercessory prayer in Chapter 9. He spent some time studying the prophecies of Jeremiah, and when found in prayer, the Angel Gabriel appears again and expounds to him the meaning of the 70-week exile of Israel predicted by Jeremiah.

Daniel 9:24 *Seventy weeks are determined upon thy people and upon thy holy city, to finish the transgression, and to make an end of sins, and to make reconciliation for iniquity, and to bring in everlasting righteousness, and to seal up the vision and prophecy, and to anoint the most Holy.*

The term "weeks" is really the Hebrew word for "sevens." So, seventy-sevens are decreed upon the house of Israel. The purpose of the sevens is to bring full chastisement on the Jewish nation for her sins and transgressions against God. When this judgment is fully exhausted, the "everlasting righteousness" and the "anointing of the Most Holy" will be brought in and, obviously, speaks of the return of Jesus.

Daniel 9:25 *Know therefore and understand, [that] from the going forth of the commandment to restore and to build Jerusalem unto the Messiah the Prince [shall be] seven weeks, and threescore and two weeks: the street shall be built again, and the wall, even in troublous times.*

The command to restore Jerusalem was given by King Cyrus while Daniel yet served under him. The angel gives the interpretive key what is the duration in years of the seventy-sevens. The period from Cyrus command to the crucifixion of Jesus was sixty-two sevens (62 x 7 = 430). The time from Cyrus command to the crucifixion of Jesus was approximately that period of time.

Notice, however, that there are seven other weeks mentioned that will add up to 69, leaving one week or seventy-sevens of years to deal with. So the understanding from Gabriel of these seventy-sevens is divided into three parts--62 weeks of years from Cyrus decree to rebuild Jerusalem to the death of Jesus, seven other weeks of years to be dealt with, and one other separate week of years to locate and identify in the prophetic time table.

Daniel 9:26 *And after threescore and two weeks shall Messiah be cut off, but not for himself: and the people of the prince that shall come shall destroy the city and the sanctuary; and the end thereof [shall be] with a flood, and unto the end of the war desolations are determined.*

This verse gives some insight into the second period of seven-sevenths which would equal 49 years. The verse speaks of the Messiah being cut off which answers to the crucifixion of Jesus. The next mention is of the "people of the prince" that is to come. In view of the fact that they destroy the city and the sanctuary, it can be assumed that this prince is the Antichrist, the little horn of the earlier vision. So, the explanation of the 70 years indicated the first 62-week period being fulfilled at the crucifixion and then shifts attention to the end times yet to be fulfilled. This would seem to say that the seventy-sevens (or 49 years) and the seventieth week or seven-year period are yet to be fulfilled in our time.

Why the Gap Between the Crucifixion and the End Time

Daniel was prophesied to about Israel, and from 70 A.D. to 1948, Israel had not been a nation. From the crucifixion to 70 A.D., Jesus gave the Jews time to receive Him through the early church even though they had rejected Him personally. When the dispensation of ministry through Paul turned to the Gentiles, Israel had by then fully "cut off the Messiah" and, consequently, condemned themselves. So, the second period of time (seven sevens or 49 years) would seem to begin to be reckoned again when the nation of Israel was reestablished.

On the basis of that understanding, 1997 is the conclusion of the second period of years in Daniel's weeks. Please note that this is only a dim insight into a possible unfolding of prophetic events. Date-setters have never been accurate before, and this study is not trying to join those unfortunate, misguided ones. This is merely an attempt to give a linear perspective on end-time events that will take place at a date and time that from all accounts will likely take place on our lifetime.

Therefore, the "prince that shall come" could very likely come into full power in the next many years. Furthermore, since he will destroy the temple as well as Jerusalem, it may be expected that the temple will be rebuilt in the next five years. For the temple to be rebuilt, however, remember that the Mosque built on the site of the Temple Mount would have to be destroyed and the location taken over by the Jews. If this happens, there will be great instability in the Middle East. It should also indicate that the liberal government in Israel at this writing will be replaced by an ultraconservative government willing to take such extreme measures.

One note here: It is possible that the temple spoken of here is not a literal building but the temple of the corporate church. This would give all these events a fulfillment in the global, corporate church rather than being centered in geographical Israel. In either case the development of the Antichrist regime will no doubt be similar to what is discussed (and the timing would be similar as well) when the outpouring of the latter rain movement in 1948 would be compared to the reestablishing of the order of God's spiritual nation in the church.

Daniel 9:27 *And he shall confirm the covenant with many for one week: and in the midst of the week he shall cause the sacrifice and the oblation to cease, and for the overspreading of abominations he shall make [it] desolate, even until the consummation, and that determined shall be poured upon the desolate.*

This prince will confirm the covenant for one week. Notice that the 62 weeks and the 70th week are mentioned but not the seven-sevens. It is assumed that when the final week is occurring, the 49-year period is already fulfilled. This verse then deals with the final week. This prince, the leader of the E.C., will make a covenant between many nations in regard to the Middle East and Israel. If this covenant marks the beginning of the 70th week and the 70th week is preceded by the seven-sevens (49 years beginning in 1948), then this European leader will initiate a peace accord in the Middle East.

The verse says that in the middle of that seven-year period of time the prince will take some action to alter the restored Jewish observances in the new temple. It is possible he will do this as a gambit to present himself as a new Mohammed or Messiah to the Christian/Moslem/Jewish religions. The result of the Antichrist interfering with Jewish worship and the Israeli reaction precipitates a time of great devastation in the world and is discussed in greater detail in other verses. It is interesting, however, that 3 ½ years (the other ½ of the 70th week) would conclude the calculation in the years following the year 2000.

Chapter Forty-five: The End Times (Part 6)

The following Scripture seems to bear out the prophetic significance of the years following the year 2000 and the period of time of the new millennia.

Hosea 6:1-3 *Come, and let us return unto the LORD: for he hath torn, and he will heal us; he hath smitten, and he will bind us up. (v. 2) After two days will he revive us: in the third day he will raise us up, and we shall live in his sight. (v. 3) Then shall we know, [if] we follow on to know the LORD: his going forth is prepared as the morning; and he shall come unto us as the rain, as the latter [and] former rain unto the earth.*

Peter said in II Peter 3:8: ". . . beloved, be not ignorant of this one thing, that one day [is] with the Lord as a thousand years, and a thousand years as one day." If the 2000-year days are reckoned from the death, burial, and resurrection of Jesus, then we have experienced the first two days already.

The church was torn and smitten in the first day. The first thousand years of the church landed it squarely in the dark ages in almost total apostasy. In the second day he healed us and bound us up. After 1000 A.D. the reformers gained power, and every aspect of church life was transformed in and out of the historic church. The binding up could be viewed as the charismatic renewal that has unified believers from all strains of the Christian faith. After two days it says we will be revived and walk in His sight. This speaks of the visible return of Jesus after the year 2000. It also speaks of tremendous revival in the church and a great end-time outpouring of the Holy Spirit.

<u>The Vision of the Period of Time Between the Old and New Testaments</u>

Daniel 11:5 through 11:35 address events that took place in the period of silence between the Old and New Testaments. His final visions deal largely with events that have already come to pass. The remaining verses of Chapter 11 through Chapter 12 deal with future events. The

past prophecies are included here as an example of the stunning accuracy of Bible prophecy. As surely as these words have come to pass, so will the remaining events inexorably come to pass.

Daniel 11:2 *And now will I shew thee the truth. Behold, there shall stand up yet three kings in Persia; and the fourth shall be far richer than [they] all: and by his strength through his riches he shall stir up all against the realm of Grecia.*

The three kings that ruled after Darius were Cyrus Cambisus, Darius Hystapys, and Xerxes. Xerses invaded Greece and "stirred up all the realm of Greece." He was defeated at Salamis.

Daniel 11:3 *And a mighty king shall stand up, that shall rule with great dominion, and do according to his will.*

This mighty King was Alexander the Great. He established his dominion in Greece, Asia Minor, Syria, and Egypt.

Daniel 11:4 *And when he shall stand up, his kingdom shall be broken, and shall be divided toward the four winds of heaven; and not to his posterity, nor according to his dominion which he ruled: for his kingdom shall be plucked up, even for others beside those.*

Alexander was cut down in his prime. Because he left no heir, his kingdom was divided between four of his military leaders.

Daniel 11:5 *And the king of the south shall be strong, and [one] of his princes; and he shall be strong above him, and have dominion; his dominion [shall be] a great dominion.*

Ptolemy was given Egypt, becoming the king of the South. Seluecus Nicator was one of Ptolemy's princes, or subordinates, and took rule of the North, naming it Seleucia.

Daniel 11:6 *And in the end of years they shall join themselves together; for the king's daughter of the south shall come to the king of the north to make an agreement: but she shall not retain the power of the arm;*

neither shall he stand, nor his arm: but she shall be given up, and they that brought her, and he that begat her, and he that strengthened her in [these] times.

There was a marriage between Ptolemy II's daughter, Berenice, and Antiochus II, a successor to the Seleucian crown. But this king was murdered by his first wife, Lucia, who installed her son Antiochus III on the throne. She then had Berenice murdered.

Daniel 11:7 *But out of a branch of her roots shall [one] stand up in his estate, which shall come with an army, and shall enter into the fortress of the king of the north, and shall deal against them, and shall prevail.*

Berenice's brother was the Egyptian king, Ptolemy III. In revenge for his sister's death, he invaded Seleucia and took much spoil.

Daniel 11:8-9 *And shall also carry captives into Egypt their gods, with their princes, [and] with their precious vessels of silver and of gold; and he shall continue [more] years than the king of the north. (v. 9) So the king of the south shall come into [his] kingdom, but shall return into his own land.*

Antiochus III invaded Egypt but was defeated.

Daniel 11:10-11 *But his sons shall be stirred up, and shall assemble a multitude of great forces: and [one] shall certainly come, and overflow, and pass through: then shall he return, and be stirred up, [even] to his fortress. (v. 11) And the king of the south shall be moved with choler, and shall come forth and fight with him, [even] with the king of the north: and he shall set forth a great multitude; but the multitude shall be given into his hand.*

Antiochus is again defeated.

Daniel 11:12-13 *[And] when he hath taken away the multitude, his heart shall be lifted up; and he shall cast down [many] ten thousands: but he shall not be strengthened [by it]. (v. 13) For the king of the north* *shall return, and shall set forth a multitude greater than the former, and shall certainly come after certain years with a great army and with much riches.*

Antiochus returned 14 years later with Seleucius III to do battle with Ptolemy II.

Daniel 11:14 *And in those times there shall many stand up against the king of the south: also the robbers of thy people shall exalt themselves to establish the vision; but they shall fall.*

Antiochus engaged Jewish mercenaries in the invasion.

Daniel 11:15 *So the king of the north shall come, and cast up a mount, and take the most fenced cities: and the arms of the south shall not withstand, neither his chosen people, neither [shall there be any] strength to withstand.*

Antiochus defeated Egypt and carried the invasion to the capital of Alexandria. Egypt never fully recovered from this defeat.

Daniel 11:16 *But he that cometh against him shall do according to his own will, and none shall stand before him: and he shall stand in the glorious land, which by his hand shall be consumed.*

As a result of this victory, Antiochus III gains a footing in Palestine, dividing Ptolemaic possessions with the king of Macedonia.

Daniel 11:17 *He shall also set his face to enter with the strength of his whole kingdom, and upright ones with him; thus shall he do: and he shall give him the daughter of women, corrupting her: but she shall not stand [on his side], neither be for him.*

Antiochus gave his daughter, Cleopatra, in marriage to Ptolemy V hoping to get full control of Egypt, but she did not stand with her father.

Daniel 11:18 *After this shall he turn his face unto the isles, and shall* *take many: but a prince for his own behalf shall cause the reproach offered by him to cease; without his own reproach he shall cause [it] to turn upon him.*

In anger Antiochus turned and invaded Greece and Asia Minor but was defeated by the Roman army at Magnesia in 190 B.C.

Daniel 11:19 *Then he shall turn his face toward the fort of his own land: but he shall stumble and fall, and not be found.*

Returning to Seleucia, Antiochus died.

Daniel 11:20-21 *Then shall stand up in his estate a raiser of taxes [in] the glory of the kingdom: but within few days he shall be destroyed, neither in anger, nor in battle. (v. 21) And in his estate shall stand up a vile person, to whom they shall not give the honor of the kingdom: but he shall come in peaceably, and obtain the kingdom by flatteries.*

Antiochus Epiphanes rose up and took the throne by treachery. He was not the eldest or in line for the throne. He was, therefore, secretly despised.

Daniel 11:22-25 *And with the arms of a flood shall they be overflown from before him, and shall be broken; yea, also the prince of the covenant. (v. 23) And after the league [made] with him he shall work deceitfully: for he shall come up, and shall become strong with a small people. (v. 24) He shall enter peaceably even upon the fattest places of the province; and he shall do [that] which his fathers have not done, nor his fathers' fathers; he shall scatter among them the prey, and spoil, and riches: [yea], and he shall forecast his devices against the strong holds, even for a time. (v. 25) And he shall stir up his power and his courage against the king of the south with a great army; and the king of the south shall be stirred up to battle with a very great and mighty army; but he shall not stand: for they shall forecast devices against him.*

Antiochus Epiphanes overthrew Egypt by force and by treachery.

Daniel 11:26 *Yea, they that feed of the portion of his meat shall destroy him, and his army shall overflow: and many shall fall down slain.*

Ptolemy VI was betrayed to Antiochus Ephiphanes by his own subjects.

Daniel 11:27 *And both these kings' hearts [shall be] to do mischief, and they shall speak lies at one table; but it shall not prosper: for yet the end [shall be] at the time appointed.*

Under guise of friendship these two kings continued to vie with each other.

Daniel 11:28 *Then shall he return into his land with great riches; and his heart [shall be] against the holy covenant; and he shall do [exploits], and return to his own land.*

On returning to Seleucia, Antiochus attacked Jerusalem, killing 80,000, taking 40,000, and selling another 40,000 into slavery.

Daniel 11:29 *At the time appointed he shall return, and come toward the south; but it shall not be as the former, or as the latter.*

At a later time Antiochus again invaded Egypt.

Daniel 11:30 *For the ships of Chittim shall come against him: therefore he shall be grieved, and return, and have indignation against the holy covenant: so shall he do; he shall even return, and have intelligence with them that forsake the holy covenant.*

But he was turned back by the Roman naval fleet who sided with Ptolemy VI.

Daniel 11:31 *And arms shall stand on his part, and they shall pollute the sanctuary of strength, and shall take away the daily [sacrifice], and they shall place the abomination that maketh desolate.*

Antiochus vented his anger by sacking Jerusalem on his return and desecrating the temple.

Daniel 11:32 *And such as do wickedly against the covenant shall he corrupt by flatteries: but the people that do know their God shall be strong, and do [exploits].*

He was aided and abetted by apostate Jews. But the Maccabean brothers carried out great exploits at that time.

Daniel 11:33-35 *And they that understand among the people shall instruct many: yet they shall fall by the sword, and by flame, by captivity, and by spoil, [many] days. (v. 34) Now when they shall fall, they shall be holpen with a little help: but many shall cleave to them with flatteries. (v. 35) And [some] of them of understanding shall fall, to try them, and to purge, and to make [them] white, [even] to the time of the end: because [it is] yet for a time appointed.*

This last verse seems to speak of a revival of repentance that prepared Israel for the coming of the Messiah. The remaining verses of this chapter and Chapter 12 seem to deal with events yet in the future.

The difficult thing in this unfolding of prophesied events that are now past is in finding the break-off point where past history concludes in the prophetic account and future history remains yet to unfold. The verses here, however, seem to indicate the break-off point with the mention of the "appointed time" that is a catch phrase in the Scriptures for the end times.

The Northern King in the Appointed Time: The Coming of the Antichrist

Daniel 11:36 *And the king shall do according to his will; and he shall exalt himself, and magnify himself above every god, and shall speak marvelous things against the God of gods, and shall prosper till the indignation be accomplished: for that that is determined shall be done.*

The subject discussed here is the king of the North at the appointed time. The northern kingdom then is a type and foreshadowing of the Antichrist government. He receives power and prospers while the full judgment of God against the nation of Israel is fulfilled. The point that he will magnify himself above every god indicates that he may present himself as a new prophet of a hybrid religion embracing Christianity, Islam, and Judaism combined.

Daniel 11:37 *Neither shall he regard the God of his fathers, nor the desire of women, nor regard any god: for he shall magnify himself above all.*

Whatever his background, he will have no regard for any religion because he will see himself as the new Messiah.

Daniel 11:38 *But in his estate shall he honour the God of forces: and a god whom his fathers knew not shall he honour with gold, and silver, and with precious stones, and pleasant things.*

His religion will be power-centered and involve a message of prosperity and material blessing.

Daniel 11:39 *Thus shall he do in the most strong holds with a strange god, whom he shall acknowledge [and] increase with glory: and he shall cause them to rule over many, and shall divide the land for gain.*

He will evangelize this new religion with great aggression and will incorporate existing economic, religious, and military structures into his organization and philosophy. He will offer power and dominion. He will divide the land for gain. This could point to his annexation of three European nations into one mighty nation in the E.C.

Daniel 11:40 *And at the time of the end shall the king of the south push at him: and the king of the north shall come against him like a whirlwind, with chariots, and with horsemen, and with many ships; and he shall enter into the countries, and shall overflow and pass over.*

These kings could be represented by the Commonwealth of Nations that was the Soviet Russia combined with Arab and Egyptian forces coming against him to no avail.

Daniel 11:41 *He shall enter also into the glorious land, and many [countries] shall be overthrown: but these shall escape out of his hand, [even] Edom, and Moab, and the chief of the children of Ammon.*

As a result of his victories, he will occupy Palestine, but some of the people will escape harm.

Daniel 11:42-43 *He shall stretch forth his hand also upon the countries: and the land of Egypt shall not escape. (v. 43) But he shall have power over the treasures of gold and of silver, and over all the precious things of Egypt: and the Libyans and the Ethiopians [shall be] at his steps.*

These nations will be by his side, and he will also amass a great economic power base.

Daniel 11:44 *But tidings out of the east and out of the north shall trouble him: therefore he shall go forth with great fury to destroy, and utterly to make away many.*

This could point again to Russia and also China that will bring military forces against him, and as a result, he will forego economic pressure in favor of outright military assault of his objectives.

Daniel 11:45 *And he shall plant the tabernacles of his palace between the seas in the glorious holy mountain; yet he shall come to his end, and none shall help him.*

Daniel 12:1 *And at that time shall Michael stand up, the great prince which standeth for the children of thy people: and there shall be a time of trouble, such as never was since there was a nation [even] to that same time: and at that time thy people shall be delivered, every one that shall be found written in the book.*

This mention of Michael could be a type of Jesus Christ corresponding with the mention of His intervention at this time in Daniel's other prophecies.

Daniel 12:2-7 *And many of them that sleep in the dust of the earth shall awake, some to everlasting life, and some to shame [and] everlasting contempt. (v. 3) And they that be wise shall shine as the brightness of the firmament; and they that turn many to righteousness as the stars forever and ever. (v. 4) But thou, O Daniel, shut up the words, and seal the book, [even] to the time of the end: many shall run to and fro, and knowledge shall be increased. (v. 5) Then I Daniel looked, and, behold, there stood other two, the one on this side of the bank of the river, and the other on that side of the bank of the river. (v. 6) And [one] said to the man clothed in linen, which [was] upon the waters of the river, How long [shall it be to] the end of these wonders? (v. 7) And I heard the man clothed in linen, which [was] upon the waters of the river, when he held up his right hand and his left hand unto heaven, and sware by him that liveth for ever that [it shall be] for a time, times, and an half; and when he shall have accomplished to scatter the power of the holy people, all these [things] shall be finished.*

The final military conquest of this ruler will cause Jesus to take action, and he will be broken "without human hand." The time period from his final invasion to his complete overthrow will be three and one-half years.

Daniel 12:8-11 *And I heard, but I understood not: then said I, O my Lord, what [shall be] the end of these [things]? (v. 9) And he said, Go thy way, Daniel: for the words [are] closed up and sealed till the time of the end. (v. 10) Many shall be purified, and made white, and tried; but the wicked shall do wickedly: and none of the wicked shall understand; but the wise shall understand. (v. 11) And from the time [that] the daily [sacrifice] shall be taken away, and the abomination that maketh desolate set up, [there shall be] a thousand two hundred and ninety days.*

Again, here is the mention of the cessation of daily sacrifice. This ruler will take Jerusalem by force and impose his Messiahship on the Christian, Islamic, and Jewish world. He will sustain his rule for exactly three and one-half years, which if our dates are correct would conclude in the years following the year 2000 and the advent of the new millennia.

Daniel 12:12 *Blessed [is] he that waiteth, and cometh to the thousand three hundred and five and thirty days.*

The blessing here is the inauguration of the millennial reign of Christ.

Daniel 12:13 *But go thou thy way till the end [be]: for thou shalt rest, and stand in thy lot at the end of the days.*

As stated before, this interpretation of these events is highly subjective and could be totally skewed from the perfect meaning of these verses. But at this time and from my perspective, these are the events that suggest, themselves, comparing prophetic predictions and time spans with current events. All these things should be held loosely but not taken lightly. While the specifics may change, the general understanding that we are living in the last days and could very possibly live to witness these cataclysmic events is undeniable.

Let us be ready and watchful and fall out in the scheme of things in cooperation with the kingdom of God and not be deceived or misled by the forces contrary to God's glorious purpose--because the end of it all is the establishment of the kingdom in righteousness and grace for eternity. Amen.

Chapter Forty-six: Overcoming the World

The Judgment of Satan's World System

In John 12 Jesus is beginning to prepare His disciples for His death and crucifixion. In the midst of gathering storms of unpopularity, Jesus declares immanent victory and the establishment of the kingdom of God.

John 12:31 *Now is the judgment of this world: now shall the prince of this world be cast out.*

Jesus is not speaking here of the last judgment. He is making an imperative statement about a judgment that was being made at that time 2000 years ago. At the end of eternity God will judge:

Mankind

Matthew 12:36 *But I say unto you, That every idle word that men shall speak, they shall give account thereof in the day of judgment.*

His church

Romans 14:10 *But why dost thou judge thy brother? or why dost thou set at nought thy brother? for we shall all stand before the judgment seat of Christ.*

The angels

I Corinthians 6:3 *Know ye not that we shall judge angels? how much more things that pertain to this life?*

The physical creation

II Peter 3:10 *But the day of the Lord will come as a thief in the night; in the which the heavens shall pass away with a great noise, and the elements shall melt with fervent heat, the earth also and the works that are therein shall be burned up.*

All of these will be judged at the end of time. The "world" spoken of here was already judged 2000 years ago. The term "world" here is from the Greek word "cosmos." It is used to describe a group or aggregate of systems that make up civilization as we know it. Cosmos in the Scriptures is used to describe:

<u>The material universe</u>

Acts 17:14 *And then immediately the brethren sent away Paul to go as it were to the sea: but Silas and Timotheus abode there still.*

<u>The inhabitants of the earth</u>

John 3:16 *For God so loved the world, that he gave his only begotten Son, that whosoever believeth in him should not perish, but have everlasting life.*

The whole arena of "worldly affairs" includes the whole circle of worldly goods, endowments, riches, advantages, and pleasures including the collective activity of all human affairs at every level from the family unit to the global scale.

I Corinthians 7:33-34 *But he that is married careth for the things that are of the world, how he may please [his] wife. (v. 34) There is difference [also] between a wife and a virgin. The unmarried woman careth for the things of the Lord, that she may be holy both in body and in spirit: but she that is married careth for the things of the world, how she may please [her] husband.*

Galatians 4:3 *Even so we, when we were children, were in bondage under the elements of the world.*

Colossians 2:20 *Wherefore if ye be dead with Christ from the rudiments of the world, why, as though living in the world, are ye subject to ordinances.*

The world that was judged 2000 years ago was the organized, orderly, planned, satanic system working invisibly behind the tangible systems and governments of the world.

The word "judge" here is the same root word for the English word "crisis." Jesus is stating here that His impending death would bring the world into a final, ultimate crisis or sentence, judgment, condemnation, and punishment.

John 12:32-33 *And I, if I be lifted up from the earth, will draw all [men] unto me. (v. 33) This he said, signifying what death he should die.*

In verse 31 Jesus depicts the downfall of the domain of darkness and its prince, and in verse 32 he predicts the rise of the Kingdom through His death. Jesus gives us the key to overcoming the powers of darkness in the earth and went to the cross in faith. His faith in the Father and what He knew about the Father assured Him that even though He went down into hell itself that the Father would be faithful to His promise. The following verse shows the promise that Jesus laid hold of and gave Him faith to overcome death itself and, thereby, overthrow the world system and break its grip on mankind.

John 12:24 *Verily, verily, I say unto you, Except a corn of wheat fall into the ground and die, it abideth alone: but if it die, it bringeth forth much fruit.*

This verse indicates Jesus' understanding of how (by dying) He could live and defeat the enemy. His willing death activated the law of seedtime and harvest found in Genesis.

Genesis 8:22 *While the earth remaineth, seedtime and harvest, and cold and heat, and summer and winter, and day and night shall not cease.*

The world that you live in is like a field. God created the earth neutral. He determined that it would take on whatever character Adam imparted to it.

Matthew 13:38 *The field is the world; the good seed are the children of* *the kingdom; but the tares are the children of the wicked [one].*

Whatever you plant in the earth it will produce. God planted His Son in the earth and reaped many sons and daughters into His family. This is because, according to the law of seedtime and harvest, the character of the seed determines the quality of the harvest.

Genesis 1:11 *And God said, Let the earth bring forth grass, the herb yielding seed, [and] the fruit tree yielding fruit after his kind, whose seed [is] in itself, upon the earth: and it was so.*

Once the growth cycle has begun, it will continue into perpetuity--one generation of planting begets another. Therefore, when Adam allowed the curse to be planted in the earth, the curse has been reproduced through Adam's seed since the garden.

Romans 5:12 *Wherefore, as by one man sin entered into the world, and death by sin; and so death passed upon all men, for that all have sinned.*

At one time a vine was imported to Mississippi to serve some agricultural purpose. Eventually, what began with one or two cuttings mushroomed into a growth of this plant that literally covers hundreds, perhaps thousands, of square acres in Mississippi. So it was with Adam: One man exercised God's law of harvest to his own hurt and brought a curse down on a whole race of men and the planet upon which they live.

Likewise, Jesus exercised this same law to bring the same race Adam cursed under His blessing. For you to receive the benefit of this life requires that you plant yourself into the kingdom of God even as God's Son planted Himself into the domain of darkness. This explains the next verse.

John 12:25 *He that loveth his life shall lose it; and he that hateth his life in this world shall keep it unto life eternal.*

Jesus is not saying that we should hate our life but that we should hate our life "in this world . . . " or in this cosmos (or system) behind which operates the mind of Satan. The world as we know it is designed to meet the agenda of the one who designed it--Satan. According to Colossians 3:1-3, your life is "hid with Christ in God . . . " because you hate the life that you live and are subjected to this world.

Colossians 3:1-3 *If ye then be risen with Christ, seek those things which are above, where Christ sitteth on the right hand of God. (v. 2) Set your affection on things above, not on things on the earth. (v. 3) For ye are dead, and your life is hid with Christ in God.*

Satan's ploy, however, is to seduce you and deceive you into withdrawing your life from committing to the kingdom of God. This is the same thing he did to Jesus. Jesus came to invest Himself into the domain of darkness. Satan tried to tempt Him to withdraw back to heaven before Jesus could reap a harvest.

Luke 4:10-12 *For it is written, He shall give his angels charge over thee, to keep thee: (v. 11) And in [their] hands they shall bear thee up, lest at any time thou dash thy foot against a stone. (v. 12) And Jesus answering said unto him, "It is said, Thou shalt not tempt the Lord thy God."*

Because of this strategy of Satan, the believer should be diligent to identify each element of the world system and the mind at work behind it and refuse to be conformed by it.

Romans 12:1 *I beseech you therefore, brethren, by the mercies of God, that ye present your bodies a living sacrifice, holy, acceptable unto God, [which is] your reasonable service.*

James 1:27 *Pure religion and undefiled before God and the Father is this, To visit the fatherless and widows in their affliction, [and] to keep himself unspotted from the world.*

Chapter Forty-seven: Overcoming the World

Exposing Satan's Strategies

In Chapter 46 we saw the importance of understanding our adversary. Paul stated once that, "We are not ignorant of his devices . . . ." We can also learn from the military minds, who plan by a primary strategy of battle, by the maxim, "Know thy enemy." We see that the world as it is described in the Scriptures is a collection of systems designed by Satan to draw man away from God. These systems include the economy, politics, arts, education, etc. If we are to be "in the world and not of it," the conclusion is that we must learn to identify every inroad that Satan's system would make into our lives.

Before the Fall

Before the fall there was no "world system," no "cosmos." With the fall, however, Satan brought to the earth an order that he conceived, and civilization as we know it was founded with that system. Because it was created and designed by Satan himself, the conclusion here is that the world as a society is inherently evil.

Daniel 2:44-45 *And in the days of these kings shall the God of heaven set up a kingdom, which shall never be destroyed: and the kingdom shall not be left to other people, [but] it shall break in pieces and consume all these kingdoms, and it shall stand for ever. (v. 45) Forasmuch as thou sawest that the stone was cut out of the mountain without hands, and that it brake in pieces the iron, the brass, the clay, the silver, and the gold; the great God hath made known to the king what shall come to pass hereafter: and the dream [is] certain, and the interpretation thereof sure.*

The world as we know it will not continue into perpetuity. From the time of the fall, God has been pursuing a plan by which the world order will be overthrown. He will establish His kingdom as a physical as well as a spiritual reality in the earth. This is the very prayer we are taught to pray, "Thy kingdom come . . ." As believers, we are ambassadors of the coming kingdom in the midst of the current world system which is passing away.

II Corinthians 5:20 *Now then we are ambassadors for Christ, as though God did beseech [you] by us: we pray [you] in Christ's stead, be ye reconciled to God.*

Philippians 2:15 *That ye may be blameless and harmless, the sons of God, without rebuke, in the midst of a crooked and perverse nation, among whom ye shine as lights in the world.*

Revelation 11:15 *And the seventh angel sounded; and there were great voices in heaven, saying, The kingdoms of this world are become [the kingdoms] of our Lord, and of his Christ; and he shall reign forever and ever.*

It is easy to point at music or the arts and identify Satan's strategy to draw us away from God. What about the seeming harmless things? What about commerce or medicine or even religion itself? At their core all these are components of a system of demonic design intended to draw us away from God.

James 1:27 *Pure religion and undefiled before God and the Father is this, To visit the fatherless and widows in their affliction, [and] to keep himself unspotted from the world.*

Romans 12:1-2 *I beseech you therefore, brethren, by the mercies of God, that ye present your bodies a living sacrifice, holy, acceptable unto God, [which is] your reasonable service. (v. 2) And be not conformed to this world: but be ye transformed by the renewing of your mind, that ye may prove what [is] that good, and acceptable, and perfect, will of God.*

II Timothy 2:4 *No man that warreth entangleth himself with the affairs of [this] life; that he may please him who hath chosen him to be a soldier.*

Satan knows well that to try to ensnare real Christians through things that are positively sinful is vain and futile. They will usually sense the danger and elude him. Understand that there are entanglements in life that may not appear openly sinful, but they are, nevertheless, very worldly and will draw us away from God.

Christians will instinctively disapprove when mention is made of a club or a gambling joint. However, in dealing with things that may not appear openly sinful yet are nonetheless worldly, our reaction can be unsure. Do you understand that all our involvements in this life are in an atmosphere that is toxic to our spiritual health? Even things that are necessary to everyday life, there can be found the strategy of Satan working to draw us away from God. The Scriptures teach that whatever we put our hand to will prosper, but we must be aware that almost everything we touch brings the influence of the world into our lives.

John 17:15-17 *I pray not that thou shouldest take them out of the world, but that thou shouldest keep them from the evil. (v. 16) They are not of the world, even as I am not of the world. (v. 17) Sanctify them through thy truth: thy word is truth.*

Concerning the World Order

The following observations can be made about the civilization in which we live. The world by its nature is hostile to God.

I Corinthians 1:21 *For after . . . the world by wisdom knew not God, it pleased God by the foolishness of preaching to save them that believe.*

Those who believe are being saved from what?—The world? Peter preached salvation from sin and Satan and also from the world system.

Acts 2:40 *And with many other words did he testify and exhort, saying, Save yourselves from this untoward generation.*

John 15:18 *If the world hate you, ye know that it hated me before it* *[hated] you.*

If we are acceptable to the world and esteemed by the world, it is because we are of the world. Understand that there is a difference between what is worldly and what is sinful. The systems of the world are designed to first entice you, enslave you, and ultimately draw you away from God. The entire world system or human civilization as we know reflects the supernatural architecture of Satan himself with a view to drawing man away from God.

John 14:17 *[Even] the Spirit of truth; whom the world cannot receive, because it seeth him not, neither knoweth him: but ye know him; for he dwelleth with you, and shall be in you.*

The world has no basis on which to comprehend God, His nature, or His Gospel unless God intervenes. It is inherently resistant to the things of God, and its systems are designed to operate by principles diametrically opposed to the principles of the Kingdom.

Jesus Told the Pharisees

John 7:7 *The world cannot hate you; but me it hateth, because I testify of it, that the works thereof are evil.*

The world and the Kingdom are as incompatible as light and darkness--the two cannot mix. The church has been taught to be separate from what is sinful. It has never, unfortunately, been given to understand the difference between what is sinful and what is worldly. The assumption has been that the two are synonymous, but they are not the same.

James 4:4 *Ye adulterers and adulteresses, know ye not that the friendship of the world is enmity with God? whosoever therefore will be a friend of the world is the enemy of God.*

We need to use great discretion in making covenants with unbelievers or dedicating ourselves to the systems of the world. These covenants/commitments involve everyday friendships, business dealings, marriages, and any binding relationship (such as debt or contractual agreements). This is why Jesus taught us to swear not at all, but let your yes be yes and your no be no.

John 18:36 *Jesus answered, "My kingdom is not of this world: if my kingdom were of this world, then would my servants fight, that I should not be delivered to the Jews: but now is my kingdom not from hence."*

In separating ourselves individually or as a church, we are not to use the world's methods. This is what Jerry Falwell's Moral Majority, the antiabortion lobby, and the Christian right wing in this country have failed to understand. They are using worldly tactics in an attempt to bring about a spiritual purpose. God does not fight fire with fire. He does not advocate resisting with flesh and blood or with the power of the lobby. Our battles should be fought on our knees. The prayer battle will defeat the spiritual forces manipulating our nation--then the changes will come at a heart level.

John 16:33 *These things I have spoken unto you, that in me ye might have peace. In the world ye shall have tribulation: but be of good cheer; I have overcome the world.*

Our victory comes by abiding in Him and doing what He would do if He were in our situation. He has overcome. If we do not see our enemy as already defeated, we are not abiding in Him.

I John 5:4 *For whatsoever is born of God overcometh the world: and this is the victory that overcometh the world, [even] our faith.*

Your faith is your most powerful weapon. It is your faith that activates the name of Jesus, the blood of Christ, and the word of God through your prayers.

I John 4:4 *Ye are of God, little children, and have overcome them: because greater is he that is in you, than he that is in the world.*

We overcome--not because of what we know but because of who lives in us. There is an evil intelligence behind the world systems around us.

John 12:31 *Now is the judgment of this world: now shall the prince of this world be cast out.*

Everything in the world bears to residue of the personality and presence of Satan himself (even things that may not be sinful but are inherently worldly). This is why the whole system has come under judgment.

John 14:30 *Hereafter I will not talk much with you: for the prince of this world cometh, and hath nothing in me.*

The goal of the believer is that the evil one's strategies will not be able to shape our lives.

John 5:19 *Then answered Jesus and said unto them, "Verily, verily, I say unto you, The Son can do nothing of himself, but what he seeth the Father do: for what things soever he doeth, these also doeth the Son likewise.*

This goal will be realized when, in His grace, the Father causes us to be limited in our motives and activates to His purposes--that we could say, "I only do what I see my Father do."

Chapter Forty-eight: Know Thy Enemy

We have seen on the earth that there is a system spoken of the in the New Testament as the "kosmos." This system is of Satanic design to fulfill his purpose of drawing men away from God. Satan, himself, is the ruler. In studying the first chapters of Genesis, it can be seen that Cain's descendants were the architects of civilization as we know it. They were first to use metals, build cities, develop the arts, and establish the systems of government.

In view of the origin of the world and its master, we understand that it is under judgment. The judgment of the world is the only aspect of judgment that was not reserved for the last days. The earth, the people in it, the saints, and the angels will all be judged at the last day. But as a system, the world was judged when Jesus went to the cross, died, and rose again.

We observe that as a system the world is hostile to God, His Kingdom, and His people. Satan's system operates to entrap the Christian and impede his growth in God. There is a distinction between what is worldly and what is sinful. Money, for instance, is not sinful, but the love of money is the root of all evil. Therefore, we must be aware that at every point where we are involved with the system there is an active mind behind that system working to draw us away from God. This is true in even the innocuous systems of the world that seemingly foster no open wickedness such as education, the sciences, commerce, or medicine.

Overcoming the World By Being Born of God

I John 5:4 *For whatsoever is born of God overcometh the world: and this is the victory that overcometh the world, [even] our faith.*

Without being born of God, you cannot even enter into conflict with the world. The world loves its own and will accommodate its own. The resources of the world are designed to work for those that are not born of God. First, you overcome the world by new birth. This can also apply to projects and efforts in life such as a business, a marriage, or any other affair of life. If it is not born of God and His will, it is woven out of the very fabric of defeat--it cannot do anything but fail. Therefore, the will of the Father must supersede the will of man.

Jesus' brothers wanted him to go to Jerusalem during the feast and "show Himself to the world." They did this because they were embarrassed by Him and wanted to get on with their lives. Jesus refused as He stated in John 7:7.

John 7:7 *The world cannot hate you; but me it hateth, because I testify of it, that the works thereof are evil.*

The issue of worldliness has to do with methods. Jesus' method was to do what He saw His Father do and to judge or make decisions as He heard the Father speak. His brothers were not concerned with what the Father wanted; they were motivated by a selfish purpose. It would have been a good thing for Jesus to show Himself to the world, but good works from a worldly motive will not fulfill the purpose of God. Any motivation or work set about by any other impetus than the revealed will of the Father is inherently worldly and will not prosper for the believer. For a worldly person, worldly methods and systems work well. The world, by its nature, is anathema to who the believer is by his very nature. There can be no compromise with the world--only conflict and ultimate victory.

John 15:18-20 *If the world hate you, ye know that it hated me before it [hated] you. (v. 19) If ye were of the world, the world would love his own: but because ye are not of the world, but I have chosen you out of the world, therefore the world hateth you. (v. 20) Remember the word that I said unto you, The servant is not greater than his lord. If they have persecuted me, they will also persecute you; if they have kept my saying, they will keep yours also.*

John 18:36 *Jesus answered, "My kingdom is not of this world: if my* *kingdom were of this world, then would my servants fight, that I should not be delivered to the Jews: but now is my kingdom not from hence."*

John 17:16-17 *They are not of the world, even as I am not of the world. (v. 17) Sanctify them through thy truth: thy word is truth.*

Having been born of God, the victory over the world initially comes about by who you are in Him. There are practical realities that you must deal with in order to operate in the world from the position of kingdom strength. This involves the practical application of faith.

Jesus said that we would be drawn from the world to Himself through the truth or the Word. The Word works through faith. Faith comes by hearing and hearing through the Word. The Word outside the heart of faith is absolutely inoperative. Therefore, the victorious life is lived in the contexts of a proper relationship to the Word, faith, and the Father's will.

The Word sanctifies you. That is, it draws you out of the domain of darkness and into the kingdom of light. Wherever the Word is applied, this is the effect. Consequently, wherever the world touches your life, it should be met by the spoken Word. You should speak daily God's Word over every area of your life affected or vulnerable to the world. You then draw that aspect of your life out from under any curse and into the atmosphere of God's blessing. This is how the Word works. There is a definite relationship between victory in living the Word, faith, and the Father's will.

I John 5:4 *For whatsoever is born of God overcometh the world: and this is the victory that overcometh the world, [even] our faith.*

Chapter Forty-nine: Mountain-Moving Prayer (Introduction)

Mark 11:22-24 *And Jesus answering saith unto them, "Have faith in God. (v. 23) For verily I say unto you, That whosoever shall say unto this mountain, Be thou removed, and be thou cast unto the sea; and shall not doubt in his heart, but shall believe that those things which he saith shall come to pass; he shall have whatoever he saith. (v. 24) Therefore I say unto you, What things soever ye desire, when ye pray, believe that ye receive [them], and ye shall have [them]." KJV*

The Amplified Bible reads:

(v. 23) Truly I tell you, whoever says to this mountain, Be lifted up and thrown into the sea! And does not doubt at all in his heart but believers that what he says will take place, it will be done for him. (v. 24) For this reason I am telling you, whatever you ask for in prayer, believe (trust and be confident) that it is granted to you, and you will get it.

The last series in the course dealt with overcoming the world. In it we saw that we (as believers) find ourselves in the midst of a world order organized and headed by Satan. By its very nature, this order is spiritually toxic to the Christian, and its continual influence in the life of a believer works to undermine his spiritual health and draw him away from God.

We saw that we overcome the world by faith or by placing our trust and confidence in the Father to meet the whole scope of our needs. Therefore, we refuse to become entangled in the chains of the world's ways, which would only serve to enslave us and destroy our walk with God.

If it is faith that preserves us from the world and faith that causes us to overcome the world even as it seeks to destroy us, how do we activate our faith? Faith is activated by prayer. Prayer is to faith what words are to thoughts. Faith is powerless without expression through prayer. Prayer is to faith what a firing pin is to a gun or what a fuse is to dynamite. There may indeed be power to move the mountain, but until prayers bring the power of our faith against the obstacles in our lives, nothing changes. Faith that does not find expression in prayer will languish in the heart, and that individual will suffer in life as though there were no God, no cross, and no name or blood of Jesus. This mighty arsenal is stored in the cabinet of faith or the heart of faith, but it cannot be brought to bear on the affairs of your life without prayer.

Luke 18:1 *And he spake a parable unto them [to this end], that men ought always to pray, and not to faint. KJV*

The Amplified Bible reads:

Also Jesus told them a parable to the effect that they ought always to pray and not to turn coward (faint, lose heart, and give up).

This verse reveals to us Jesus' philosophy of prayer. There are many viewpoints on prayer from every quarter in the religious realm. Some emphasize prayer greatly; some not at all. But, it is only Jesus' view on prayer that the Father promises to back up when you put it into practice.

First of all, notice that "Men ought *always* to pray . . ." not for a few minutes at bedtime, or meals, or for an hour in the morning. We should always pray. In order to do this and still go about your daily business, you have to throw out your religious concepts of prayer. Prayer is essentially to communicate with God.

Ephesians 6:18 *Praying always with all prayer and supplication in the Spirit, and watching thereunto with all perseverance and supplication for all saints.*

The Amplified Bible reads:

Pray at all times (on every occasion, in every season) in the Spirit with all manner of prayer . . .

Different kinds of prayer are appropriate for different occasions. It would not be appropriate to get on your knees on the street to pray. Jesus taught that obvious prayer should be given in the prayer closet. There is prayer that is prayed under your breath or in the back of your mind. It is possible at all times to be in communion or communication with the Father. Because He encourages us to do this, it is evident that He will be listening and answering every prayer we offer up to Him.

According to Jesus in Luke 18:1, the whole point of prayer is to gain deliverance over cowardice, fear, and failure. These problems plague us because of prayerlessness. Prayer is not a secret magical sort of thing. Prayer is a means to the end of being continually exposed to the spirit of God and directing His presence toward your needs and the needs of others.

My grandmother, Birdie Walden, coined the pithy phrase, "Much prayer, much power--little prayer, little power." You may not understand why prayer is so necessary, but if you can see that the Word emphasized it, be satisfied it is important to the Father that you continually pray. This satisfies Him. So, begin with the motive of pleasing the Father's heart, and trust that a deeper understanding of the prayer gift will come in time.

James 5:15 *And the prayer of faith shall save the sick, and the Lord shall raise him up; and if he have committed sins, they shall be forgiven him.*

Prayer changes things. Prayer is necessary because change is needed. Prayer is necessary because Satan will continually attempt to encroach into your life, health, family, or finances. Prayer is the weapon by which the spirit of God throws the enemy back and defeats his wicked purpose in your life.

Prayer is the means by which personal provision becomes personal experience. Jesus took stripes for your healing 2000 years ago. That personal provision is translated into personal experience through prayer. Heaven's resources of health, healing, salvation, deliverance, and provision are dispensed at the tap of the prayer of faith.

James 5:16 *Confess [your] faults one to another, and pray one for another, that ye may be healed. The effectual fervent prayer of a righteous man availeth much.*

Effectiveness in prayer is based on the righteousness that Jesus provided for you on Calvary. Your prayers are answered because of who Jesus is and what He did on the cross for you. Who you are or what you have done do not factor into answered prayer. The most rank failure or the most holy saint must come humbly to the altar of prayer on the basis of the blood of Christ.

James 5:17-18 *Elias was a man subject to like passions as we are, and he prayed earnestly that it might not rain: and it rained not on the earth by the space of three years and six months. (v. 18) And he prayed again, and the heaven gave rain, and the earth brought forth her fruit.*

The writer of Hebrews stresses that we have a better covenant than Elijah had under the law. Elijah's prayer was heard even though he was a man of "like passion" or "with feeling, constitution, and affections like ours . . ." He was made of the same stuff that you and I are made of; yet God answered his prayers and brought the nation of Israel to its knees. Likewise, through the better covenant of the blood of Christ, the forces of Satan ranged against you and your loved ones will be brought to their knees if you will dare to ask. Put your trust for an answer in who Jesus is and what He did without being intimidated or condemned by your own failures to live up to what you thought was necessary to receive answered prayer.

John 16:24 *Hitherto have ye asked nothing in my name: ask, and ye shall receive, that your joy may be full.*

Chapter Fifty: Mountain-Moving Prayer (Continued)

Mark 11:22-24 And Jesus anwering saith unto them, "Have faith in God. (v. 23) For verily I say unto you, That whosoever shall say unto this mountain, Be though removed, and be thou cast into the sea; and shall not doubt in his heart, but shall believe that those things which he saith shall come to pass; he shall have whatsoever he saith. (v. 24) Therefore, I say unto you, What things soever ye desire, when you pray, believe that ye receive [them], and ye shall have [them]."

The Amplified Bible reads:

And Jesus said to them, Have faith in God [constantly]. (v. 23) Truly I tell you, whoever says to this mountain, Be lifted up and thrown into the sea! And does not doubt at all in his heart but believes that what he says will take place, it will be done for him. (v. 24) For this reason I am telling you, whatever you ask for in prayer, believe (trust and be confident) that it is granted to you, and you will get it.

In the last chapter we covered the basic definition of prayer. Prayer is simply communication with God in any of several ways. We read in Luke 18:1 where Jesus taught that men should always pray to prevent fear and failure. Paul commanded in Ephesians 6:18 to pray at all times with all manner (different kinds) of prayer. We saw that prayer is necessary because of the need for change in our lives and the fact that in most cases the needed changes can only be fully effected by divine intervention. Prayer is the means that God has given us to activate our faith and bring changes into our lives.

James gave Elijah as an example of a man with passions and a disposition very common to man. His prayer life was effective because of his earnest, heart-felt prayer. Therefore, we expect our prayers to be answered on the basis of who Jesus is and what He has done for us, not on the basis of our own spirituality or performance. Even in failure you can pray boldly because you come before the Father on the basis of the blood of Christ and not your merits or performance.

Prayer in the Spirit

Paul said in Ephesians 6:18 that we should pray at all times "in the Spirit." There are two ways to do this as outlined below.

1. Pray in Tongues

Acts 2:4 *And they were all filled with the Holy Ghost, and began to speak with other tongues, as the Spirit gave them utterance.*

Where was the Spirit when He gave these people utterance? They had been in prayer in the upper room for over a month after the ascension of Jesus waiting on the Lord. Certainly these people were born again. The Spirit that filled them lived within them in their inner man.

The gift of tongues works in your prayer life as you yield your faculty of speech to your inner man in the same way you allow your mind to manipulate the speech center of your brain. Your soul lives in your mind and speaks through your mouth. The Holy Spirit lives in your heart, and when he is given control of your mouth, he fills the mind, the emotions, and the whole man and then expresses the Father's perfect will in an angelic language.

Romans 8:26 *Likewise the Spirit also helpeth our infirmities: for we know not what we should pray for as we ought: but the Spirit itself maketh intercession for us with groanings which cannot be uttered.*

I Corinthians 14:18 *I thank my God, I speak with tongues more than ye all.*

When you pray in tongues, you are praying in absolute faith. It is impossible to pray in tongues contrary to the will of God. Every prayer you pray in tongues will receive an answer without fail.

Jude 20-21 *But ye, beloved, building up yourselves on your most holy faith, praying in the Holy Ghost, (v. 21) Keep yourselves in the love of*

God, looking for the mercy of our Lord Jesus Christ unto eternal life.

Praying in the Spirit builds faith. Praying in the Spirit keeps you bathed in the love of God. Praying in the Spirit is a dynamic gift given to the church to maintain our spiritual health.

2. Pray the Word

John 6:63 *. . . the words that I speak unto you, [they] are spirit, and [they] are life.*

Another way to pray in the Spirit is to pray the Word. When you pray, the Word you are praying is absolute faith. When you pray the Word, it is impossible to pray contrary to the will of God. Every prayer you pray according to the Word will receive an answer without fail.

Hebrews 3:1 *Wherefore, holy brethren, partakers of the heavenly calling, consider the Apostle and High Priest of our profession, Christ Jesus.*

When you pray the Word, your "profession" is taken before the Father by Jesus Himself. Jesus is the Priest of your profession of faith. He takes your faith before the Father and petitions the Father to honor the Word that Jesus gave us.

Hebrews 4:14 *Seeing then that we have a great high priest, that is passed into the heavens, Jesus the Son of God, let us hold fast [our] profession.*

When Jesus ascended, He made a clear path for your prayers directly to the Father's throne. Our part is to make our profession based on the Word of God and then hold fast to it. When Jesus ascended, He passed through heaven where the spiritual battles rage.

Hebrews 10:23 *Let us hold fast the profession of [our] faith without wavering; (for he [is] faithful that promised.)*

Hebrews 10:38 *Now the just shall live by faith: but if [any man] draw back, my soul shall have no pleasure in him.*

Chapter Fifty-one: Mountain-Moving Prayer (Continued)

David's Prayer Life

To the chief Musician on Neginoth, A Psalm of David.

***Psalms 4:**1 Hear me when I call, O God of my righteousness: thou hast enlarged me [when I was] in distress; have mercy upon me, and hear my prayer.*

This is the first specific mention of prayer in the Psalms. David begins his prayer by making connection with "Hear me O God . . ." He is focusing on the Father. He is making eye contact, as it were, with Jehovah. He speaks of God and righteousness. He is coming to the Father on the basis of God's mercy and not any merit of his own. He then reminds the Lord of past deliverances and asks for God to have mercy and hear him.

***Psalms 4:2** O ye sons of men, how long [will ye turn] my glory into shame? [how long] will ye love vanity, [and] seek after leasing? Selah.*

David then speaks to his enemies. He provokes his enemies to stop and meditates on the faithfulness of God. In prayer you will also speak to God, to yourself, and to your enemies.

***James 2:19** Thou believest that there is one God; thou doest well: the devils also believe, and tremble.*

When you speak the Word of God to your enemies, you activate their faith, and they participate in their own destruction.

***Psalms 4:3** But know that the LORD hath set apart him that is godly for himself: the LORD will hear when I call unto him.*

He reminds his enemies that the Lord will hear his prayer.

Psalms 4:4 *Stand in awe, and sin not: commune with your own heart upon your bed, and be still. Selah.*

He then turns to himself and begins to speak comfort to his own heart. David continually encouraged himself in the Lord.

Psalms 103:2-5 *Bless the LORD, O my soul, and forget not all his benefits: (v. 3) Who forgiveth all thine iniquities; who healeth all thy diseases; (v. 4) Who redeemeth thy life from destruction; who crowneth thee with lovingkindness and tender mercies; (v. 5) Who satisfieth thy mouth with good [things; so that] thy youth is renewed like the eagle's.*

I Samuel 30:6 *And David was greatly distressed; for the people spake of stoning him, because the soul of all the people was grieved, every man for his sons and for his daughters: but David encouraged himself in the LORD his God.*

David took responsibility for his own spiritual well-being. You must realize that the Father has placed you largely on your own recognizance when it comes to your spiritual life and growth. You cannot leave these things to others no matter how willing they are to be your spiritual surrogate.

Psalms 4:5 *Offer the sacrifices of righteousness, and put your trust in the LORD.*

What are the sacrifices of righteousness? These are what you offer the Lord in anticipation of answered prayer.

I Corinthians 1:30 *But of him are ye in Christ Jesus, who of God is made unto us wisdom, and righteousness, and sanctification, and redemption.*

Jesus Christ is our righteousness. It is His person that gives us standing before the Father in prayer.

Psalms 4:6 *[There be] many that say, Who will shew us [any] good?*

LORD, lift thou up the light of thy countenance upon us.

David is very honest in his prayers. He does not try to con God. He further sees the person of God as the answer, not what God can give him. He is seeking the giver and not just the gift.

In the following Psalms David is quite blunt about what he wants to happen to his enemies. Is this God's will? Probably not. Was God mad at David for speaking so brashly? No, He accepted David's transparency and honesty and rewarded him for it.

Psalms 58:6 *Break their teeth, O God, in their mouth: break out the great teeth of the young lions, O LORD.*

A Psalm of David.

Psalms 35:1 *Plead [my cause], O LORD, with them that strive with me: fight against them that fight against me.*

Psalms 35:5-6, 8-9 *Let them be as chaff before the wind: and let the angel of the LORD chase [them] (v. 6) Let their way be dark and slippery: and let the angel of the LORD persecute them. (v. 8) Let destruction come upon him at unawares; and let his net that he hath hid catch himself: into that very destruction let him fall. (v. 9) And my soul shall be joyful in the LORD: it shall rejoice in his salvation.*

What did David do when his enemies were smitten?

Psalms 35:13-14 But as for me, when they were sick, my clothing [was] sackcloth: I humbled my soul with fasting; and my prayer returned into mine own bosom. (v. 14) I behaved myself as though [he had been] my friend [or] brother: I bowed down heavily, as one that mourneth [for his] mother.

David reminds God that he came to the aid of the enemies who were smitten in response to his own prayer! This is the honest, transparent, and absence of guile we must demonstrate if we expect and hope for answers in prayer. Do not roll out the King's English and try to manipulate God with fair, dishonest speech.

Psalms 4:7 *Thou hast put gladness in my heart, more than in the time [that] their corn and their wine increased.*

When it comes to provision and supply, David speaks out his confidence in God. He prays the answer and not the problem. He speaks by faith concerning his present circumstance. He is calling those things that are not as though they were.

Psalms 4:8 *I will both lay me down in peace, and sleep: for thou, LORD, only makest me dwell in safety.*

Then he prophesies his future. He puts his trust in the Lord and lays the issue to rest.

Chapter Fifty-two: Mountain-Moving Prayer (Conclusion)

John 5:17-19 *But Jesus answered them, "My Father worketh hitherto, and I work." (v. 18) Therefore the Jews sought the more to kill him, because he not only had broken the sabbath, but said also that God was his Father, making himself equal with God. (v. 19) Then answered Jesus and said unto them, "Verily, verily, I say unto you, The Son can do nothing of himself, but what he seeth the Father do: for what things soever he doeth, these also doeth the Son likewise."*

A study of the prayer life of Jesus is a study of His relationship with the Father. There are not many prayer teachings patterned after His prayer life because it was not built on religious unreality but on intimate communion with the Father. We have said that prayer is communication with the Father. Jesus demonstrates the quintessence of what that communion is like.

From this verse we can see that Jesus communed with the Father the same way you and I can commune with the Father. What He saw the Father do, He saw inwardly. He taught that the kingdom of God is within us, and His intimacy with the Father was an inward thing. God spoke to Him through His mind, His imagination, and through the eye of His human spirit--and He acted upon that revelation.

Television is a mechanical model of that part of the human spirit we call imagination. It will receive the images of whatever you watch (whatever it is tuned to will constitute your programming). Jesus tuned His inner man to the Father's thoughts, feelings, and purposes as we are taught over and again to put on the mind of Christ.

John 12:49 *For I have not spoken of myself; but the Father which sent me, he gave me a commandment, what I should say, and what I should speak.*

Philippians 2:5 *Let this mind be in you, which was also in Christ Jesus.*

Romans 12:2 *And be not conformed to this world: but be ye transformed by the renewing of your mind, that ye may prove what [is] that good, and acceptable, and perfect, will of God.*

John 10:30 *I and [my] Father are one.*

John 5:20 *For the Father loveth the Son, and sheweth him all things that himself doeth: and he will shew him greater works than these, that ye may marvel.*

The Father will not leave you in the dark if you will be sensitive enough to listen and bold enough to believe what He tells you.

Amos 3:7 *Surely the Lord GOD will do nothing, but he revealeth his secret unto his servants the prophets.*

Isaiah 45:11 *Thus saith the LORD, the Holy One of Israel, and his Maker, Ask me of things to come concerning my sons, and concerning the work of my hands command ye me.*

John 5:26-27, 30 *For as the Father hath life in himself; so hath he given to the Son to have life in himself; (v. 27) And hath given him authority to execute judgment also, because he is the Son of man. (v. 30) I can of mine own self do nothing: as I hear, I judge: and my judgment is just; because I seek not mine own will, but the will of the Father which hath sent me.*

Jesus knew His limitations. His limits or boundaries were the boundaries of His personal relationship with the Father. The power and life and authority you have as a believer is an expression of your intimacy with the Father. The increase of these things comes as an increase of intimacy with Him.

John 8:38 *I speak that which I have seen with my Father: and ye do that which ye have seen with your father.*

The universal principle governing humanity is that you are doing the works of your father. Your life is an expression of your perception of who he is, and your perception is determined by your relationship to him. These men were totally out of relationship with God and were expressing the paternity of Satan. You had no choice of earthly parents. There is one exception. By making a turn in your mind and heart toward Jesus Christ, the Father adopts you into His family, and you have an opportunity to express His life, power, and creativity as opposed to the death, destruction, and depravity of Satan.

John 10:18 *No man taketh it from me, but I lay it down of myself. I have power to lay it down, and I have power to take it again. This commandment have I received of my Father.*

When you know the voice of the Father, you know your authority extends itself within the parameters of His guidance in your life.

John 11:41 *Then they took away the stone [from the place] where the dead was laid. And Jesus lifted up [his] eyes, and said, "Father, I thank thee that thou hast heard me."*

Jesus had a perfect communion with His Father. There was no sense of asking or wondering if His Father would be there.

John 11:42 *And I knew that thou hearest me always: but because of the people which stand by I said [it], that they may believe that thou hast sent me.*

John 13:3 *Jesus knowing that the Father had given all things into his hands, and that he was come from God, and went to God.*

There was no question Jesus knew His limits, and He knew His Father.

John 14:8 *Philip saith unto him, Lord, shew us the Father, and it sufficeth us.*

Jesus knew that His life reflected the Father's nature and character.

John 14:9-10, 12-13 *Jesus saith unto him, "Have I been so long time with you, and yet hast thou not known me, Philip? he that hath seen me hath seen the Father; and how sayest thou [then], Shew us the Father? (v. 10) Believest thou not that I am in the Father, and the Father in me? the words that I speak unto you I speak not of myself: but the Father that dwelleth in me, he doeth the works. (v. 12) Verily, verily, I say unto you, He that believeth on me, the works that I do shall he do also; and greater [works] than these shall he do; because I go unto my Father. (v. 13) And whatsoever ye shall ask in my name, that will I do, that the Father may be glorified in the Son.*

It is important that we acknowledge our own limitations when approaching the Father. Answered prayer originates in an obedient heart. You may struggle and question, but this is not true doubt. God values honesty above all when you come to Him. Out of that honesty will come resultant answers that proceed from the heart of God's mercy toward you when you approach Him in humility.

ABOUT THE AUTHOR

Insert author bio text here. Insert author bio text here

Made in the USA
Middletown, DE
22 May 2021

39954384R00136